A COMPLETE CROCHET COURSE

A COMPLETE CROCHET COURSE

Muriel Kent

with 16 pages of colour photographs
and 100 line drawings

DAVID & CHARLES
Newton Abbot   London   North Pomfret (Vt)

British Library Cataloguing in Publication Data

Kent, Muriel
A complete crochet course.
1. Crocheting
I. Title
746.43'4   TT820

ISBN 0-7153-8599-2

Typeset by Typesetters (Birmingham) Limited
Smethwick, West Midlands
and printed in Great Britain
by Butler & Tanner Limited, Frome
for David & Charles (Publishers) Limited
Brunel House   Newton Abbot   Devon

Published in the United States of America
by David & Charles Inc
North Pomfret   Vermont 05053   USA

CONTENTS

INTRODUCTION

Crochet is one of the most neglected crafts and yet it can be one of the easiest and most exciting. Many people say 'I can crochet but not read a pattern' or 'I can crochet but not keep the edges straight'. This book is for them and also for those who just cannot crochet but would love to. It is also hoped that people who are most proficient will glean new ideas and be inspired to experiment with yarn or stitch or just to follow one of the many designs.

The history of crochet is obscure; flax and wool are perishable and so the evidence has disappeared, but it is one of the oldest crafts and probably came before knitting. The stitches would have been used to make shawls and blankets for warmth. During the Middle Ages when lace was so fashionable for both men and women it was discovered that crochet stitches used with fine flax or cotton could be used to produce a fast-growing fabric similar to the bobbin lace which took so long to make. This crochet lace became known as Nun's Work and the nuns taught the children how to make it in the schools.

During the First World War most women could crochet and, after knitting socks for soldiers, they produced miles of white lace for their trousseaux, edging bed linen, tablecloths and nighties whilst waiting for their menfolk to return from the front. Lace went out of fashion after the war, yet now that same lace is enjoying a revival in the antique shops. It has been bleached and laundered and offered for sale at prices which would have been unbelievable when it was made. The women of southern Europe and the Mediterranean have not deserted their craft and one only has to visit countries like Spain, Italy, Malta and Greece to discover exquisite tops and linen at ridiculously low prices.

Between the wars crochet declined in popularity and was considered old-fashioned. Only a few women could do much more than make edgings for knitted garments. In the late Fifties and Sixties, however, crochet was re-discovered in the search for something new and original. Lacy mini dresses and crocheted trouser suits became high fashion, but this revival was relatively short lived. Crochet was used for clothes with thicker yarns and not so much for decoration and was, in effect, an entirely different craft. The designers were relatively inexperienced and the patterns available were frequently incorrect and difficult to follow. Many people were disappointed with their efforts, therefore did not progress beyond the granny squares or lacy waistcoat. Hopefully this book will persuade those people to try again.

I hope very much also that teachers will use this book to introduce crochet as a school craft. In these days of education cuts a hook is the only expenditure necessary. A school appeal for oddments of yarn will, I am sure, provide plenty. The boys are often as keen as the girls and just as good or even better and the first lesson in this book should provide enough ideas to last a term.

My method of teaching is to learn only one stitch at a time. The treble comes first, concentrating on how to hold the hook in the right hand and the yarn in the left and immediately starting to make something however simple. Familiarise your pupils with the techniques of the craft before introducing all the stitches.

This complete course of crochet does not claim to be a complete book of crochet. Modern crochet is a wide, open-ended craft; new stitches and techniques are continually being discovered. This course is complete in so far as it takes readers from tying the first slip knot right through to making buttons for a finished garment. Many crochet books give details of all kinds of stitches – this book is different in that it gives few stitches and attempts to cut down and simplify everything, giving the minimum information needed to produce attractive fashionable garments and all the information required to enable the complete beginner to become a skilled worker.

I hope you will progress with hook in hand at every step and work through rather than read through the book, taking time to progress from making an easy belt or bag to a jacket or coat, absorbing information without realising it and by Lesson 6 to have a very comprehensive knowledge of the craft with the confidence to tackle anything from a commercial pattern to an exclusive garment of your own design.

ACKNOWLEDGEMENTS

I would like to thank all the people who helped with the preparation of this book, especially Lyn Arscott of Line Design who prepared the line illustrations; J. & P. Coats Ltd for their kind permission to copy the hand positions of Figs 1–4 and some of the stitch diagrams from *Learn to Crochet 1292*; Marjorie Eden for typing the manuscript and for her careful checking of the instructions; Pat Dean, Freda Leggat, Beryl Reynolds, Greta Lawrence and Beryl Eyles who helped with some of the garments; the yarn firms of Twilleys, Priory Yarns, Phildar and Patons who kindly donated materials for some of the garments; and Dave and Mary Vinall of Woolscope, Chichester, who helped by obtaining hooks and yarn. Last, but by no means least, I would like to thank my husband, Max, for all his encouragement.

ABBREVIATIONS & TERMS

	UK		USA	SYMBOLS
ch	chain			◯◯◯
sl st	slip stitch			⌒⌒
dc	double crochet	sc	single crochet	
tr	treble crochet	dc	double crochet	
htr	half treble	hdc	half double crochet	
dtr	double treble	tr	treble	
tr tr	triple treble	dtr	double treble	
quad tr	quad treble	tr tr	triple treble	

st	stitch		
tch	turning chain		
lp	loop		
yrh	yarn round hook		
inc	increase		
dec	decrease		
tog	together		
patt	pattern		
sp	space		
RtrF	raised treble front	RdeF	raised double crochet forward
RtrB	raised treble back	RdeB	raised single crochet backward
gr	group		
cl	cluster		
Tdc	Tunisian double crochet		
Ttr	Tunisian treble		
Tdtr	Tunisian double treble		
Ttr tr	Tunisian triple treble		
Tp	Tunisian purl		
Tdp tr	Tunisian dropped treble		
Tss	Tunisian stocking stitch		
Tb	Tunisian bobble		

Note: UK terms only are used throughout this book. However, as some American terms differ from the UK ones and some crochet patterns use symbols rather than abbreviations, the additional information given here may be useful, particularly when tackling continental or American patterns.

Lesson 1
BASIC TECHNIQUES

Beginners should read the book with hook and yarn in hand and work everything as presented in Lessons 1 and 2. Some stages will take much longer than others but by working consistently through the book it should be possible to progress from learning how to hold the hook and yarn to making quite intricate garments without a written pattern.

Yarn and Hook

It is much simpler to start with a thick yarn and a large hook. Mistakes are more visible and it is much easier to see the stitches. Use yarn of Aran thickness and a 6.00mm hook, or chunky thickness and a 7.00mm hook. Check the hook sizes. They were standardised in 1969 but there are many hooks of the old sizing still in use (see Appendix 1).

When the stitches have been mastered in thick yarn it is then possible to reduce the size of both yarn and hook. From fine white lace to large chunky patterns the individual stitches are the same. The variations are made by the combination of the actual stitches. Once the technique has been mastered it is possible to make anything from a fine lace bedspread taking a year or so, to a large chunky jacket in about a week. The first lesson demonstrates only the treble stitch leaving the other stitches until speed and confidence are gained. It is possible to make a fashionable jacket with only the treble (see Design 4, page 95).

Tying a Slip Knot
All crochet stitches begin with a slip knot on the hook.
1 Hold yarn in the right hand with the end hanging down.
2 Grasp end of yarn with the left hand and with the right hand wind it once round the first two fingers of the left hand.
3 Insert hook into circle of yarn and pull loop through circle and onto the hook.
4 Pull long end of yarn to tighten loop on hook.

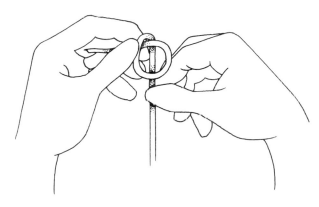

Fig 1

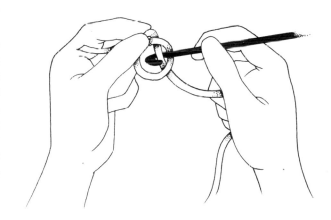

Fig 2

Holding the Yarn

Knitters who usually hold the yarn with their right hand find it difficult to change and hold it in the left for crochet but it is necessary for the left hand to control the yarn, thus allowing the latter to flow easily and smoothly from hand to hook giving speed and an even tension. With a little practice it becomes automatic, however difficult it may seem at first.

1   Hold the left hand with fingers extended and palm uppermost.
2   Hold hook and slip knot in the right hand.
3   Bring yarn between the third and fourth fingers of the left hand, over and behind the fourth finger.
4   Continue over the third finger, passing to the back between the third and second finger.
5   Relax hand, turn over and the yarn will fall over the first and second fingers.
6   Grasp the slip knot with the first finger and the thumb.

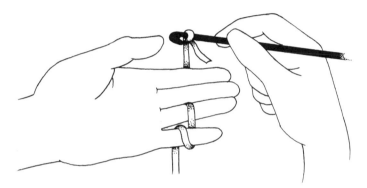

Fig 3

Making a Chain (ch)

1   Hold hook in the first finger and thumb of the right hand, supporting the hook underneath with the third finger.
2   Hold the slip knot with the first finger and thumb of the left hand. The second finger is raised to hold the yarn in position for working from the hook.
3   Move hook under the yarn and pull a loop through, yarn round hook.

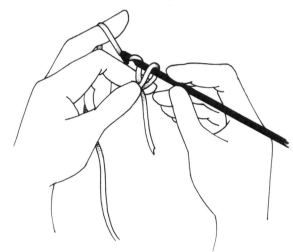

Fig 4

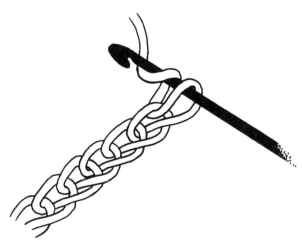

Fig 5

Repeat this movement until it becomes quite rhythmical and automatic and continue until the chain is regular and smooth. Run the first finger and thumb along the chain and notice that the front side is smooth and the back is ridged. Always work into the front of the chain and do not allow it to twist.

If your chain stitches are tight use a larger size hook returning to the original size after the chains have been worked.

Fig 6 FRONT CHAIN

Fig 7 BACK CHAIN

Treble Stitch (tr)

1   Notice that the chain is a loop with a strand passing from it to the next stitch. When working place the hook into the bottom of the chain making two threads on the hook.

2   Place yarn round hook (yrh).

3   Insert hook into 4th ch from hook.

4   yrh and pull through 1 loop (lp).

5   yrh and pull through 2lps.

6   yrh and pull through 2lps.

7   yrh and insert hook into next ch. Repeat steps 4, 5 and 6.

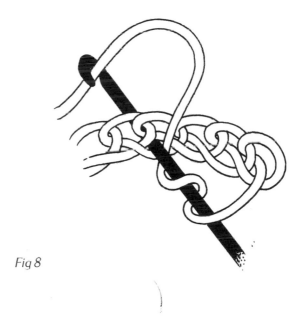

Fig 8

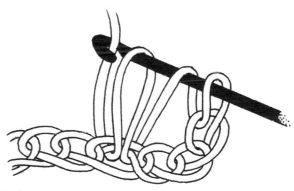

Fig 9

Fig 10

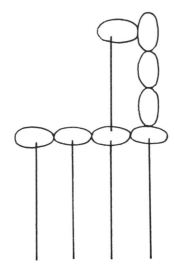

Fig 12

Fig 11

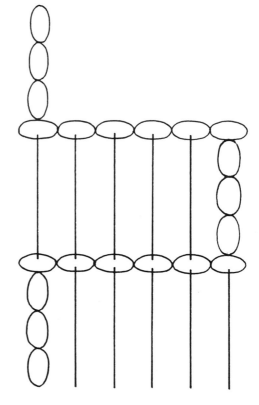

Continue working in this way to the end of the chain. Practise until your work is rhythmic and even. If it is not good enough pull it out and start again. A lot of practice at this stage will pay off later on.

Keeping the Edges Straight
1 At the end of first row of tr make 3 ch. These are called turning chain (tch). Turn work.
2 Hold tch at right angles to row completed and you will see that this 3 ch will count as the first st.
3 1 tr into the end st and 1 tr into every st to the end of the row making 1 tr into the 3rd tch of the previous row, 3 ch and turn.
4 Repeat the previous row.

The secret of keeping the work straight is to miss the first stitch of the row and to work a stitch into the top turning chain of the previous row. Always check the number of stitches every row until it automatically becomes even with the edges straight.

Fig 13

Common Mistakes

1 Two stitches into one loop especially on the first chain.

2 Missing a stitch.

3 Working the first treble into the first stitch instead of the second stitch.

4 Missing the last stitch which should be into the turning chain of the previous row.

Stitch Patterns with a Treble

When working into a stitch it means that the hook is placed from the front to the back of the work under the chain loop at the top of the treble. This gives two strands of yarn over the hook. The stitches must always be worked the same way with the hook going into the same part of the stitch every time. At the end of the row always turn the work the same way every time, either clockwise or anti-clockwise. Work four or five rows of the following and compare the different textures.

1 Insert hook into front of ch lp at top of tr.

2 Insert hook into back of ch lp at top of tr.

3 Insert hook into space between the treble bars.

Remember to work three turning chain at the end of every row.

Stitch Pattern No 1 – Tricot Stitch

Make 23ch.

Row 1 1tr into 4th ch from hook, *1ch, miss 1st, 1tr*. Repeat from * to end of row finishing with 1tr 4ch, turn.

Row 2 Work trebles over trebles and 1ch over spaces.

This stitch gives an open work mesh which can be used for weaving with yarn or ribbon (see colour illustration, page 112).

Stitch Pattern No 2 – V Stitch

Make 21ch. Miss 5ch.

Row 1 *1tr 2ch 1tr* into next st, miss 2st, repeat from * to end of row, 1tr 3ch, turn.

Repeat Row 1 throughout working 1tr 2ch 1tr into each 2ch sp.

Try one row of each colour. Use three colours and then it is not necessary to join on. Carry the new colour along the side.

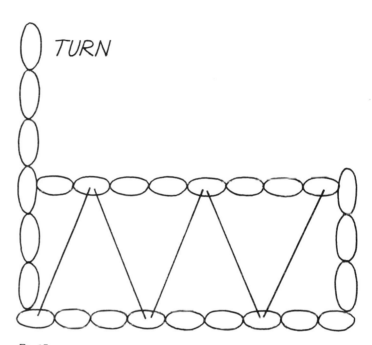

Fig 15

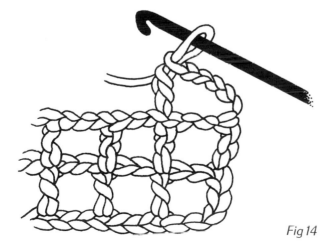

Fig 14

Stitch Pattern No 3 – 3 Trebles into 1 Space
Make 23ch.
Row 1 1tr into 4th ch from hook, and 1tr into every st, 4ch, turn (21 bars).
Row 2 3tr into 3rd sp, 3tr into every 3rd sp to end of row until 3tr remain. 1ch 1tr into tch of previous row, 3ch, turn.
Row 3 2tr into 1st sp, 3tr into every sp to end of row. Work last tr into tch instead of sp as this keeps edge straight.

This stitch is suitable for scarves and shawls.

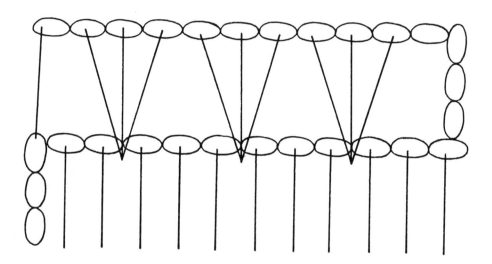

Fig 16

Stitch Pattern No 4 – Eyelet Treble
Make 23ch.
Row 1 1tr into 4th ch from hook, 1tr into every ch, 3ch, turn.
Row 2 1tr into 2nd st, *1ch, miss 1st, 1tr into next st, repeat from * to end of row finishing with 1tr into tch of previous row, 3ch, turn.
Row 3 1tr into 2nd st, *1tr into 1ch sp, 1tr into next st. Repeat from * to end of row finishing with 1tr into tch of previous row, 3ch, turn.
Rows 2 and 3 form pattern
This stitch is used for Design 9, page 101.

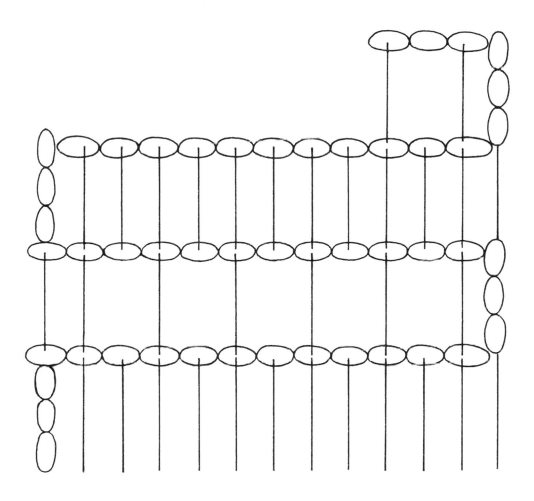

Fig 17

Stitch Pattern No 5 - A Crochet Rib Stitch
Make 20ch.
Row 1 1tr into 4th ch from hook, 1tr into every ch, 2ch, turn.
Row 2 yrh, place hook horizontally from right to left under bar of 2nd tr of previous row, yrh and pull lp through (yrh and pull through 2lps) twice, completing the tr st. This forms a RtrF (raised treble Front). yrh, take hook to back of work, coming from back insert it over bar of next tr and out to back of work, yrh and complete tr at back. This forms a RtrB (raised treble Back). Repeat these 2st to end of row.

This stitch needs only two turning chain as it is not as tall as an ordinary treble. The more rows completed the more elastic the rib becomes. If you find this stitch difficult, ask a friend to read the instructions word by word whilst you work it. When you have mastered the stitch think of Raised treble Front as knit 1 and Raised treble Back as purl 1. To give a rib st RtrF of one row is worked over RtrB of the previous row. This is the equivalent of working knit over purl and purl over knit. This stitch is used for the hat brim of Design 5, page 97. Knitters – now try the equivalent of moss stitch, knit 2 purl 2 rib, and basket stitch. (Basket stitch is explained in detail for the scarf in Design 5, page 97.)

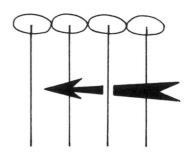

Fig 18

Hook position – horizontally in front of work, behind treble

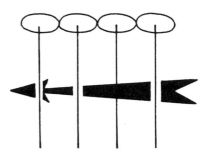

Fig 19

Hook position – horizontally behind work, in front of treble

How to Make a Fringe

For a scarf, stole or bag you might like to make a fringe to decorate the ends.

1 Wind yarn round a book. A large book for a long fringe and a paper-back for a small fringe.
2 Make strips by cutting along one side.
3 Take about 4 strands together and fold in halves to make lp. Place hook between 2tr, put lp on hook and pull through.
4 With hook pull the ends through lp and tighten.

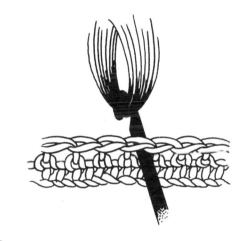

Fig 20

Fig 21

When you have finished the fringe, trim the ends straight. Experiment to see how thick you would like your fringe and use the number of strands accordingly. It pays to be generous with the fringe but it takes more yarn than you might expect.

Left-handed Crocheters

I have found that about one in ten students is left handed and in the initial stages they do experience a little difficulty. Once they have mastered how to hold the yarn their problems are over. Here are some helpful tips:

1 All working instructions must be reversed – for *left* read *right* and for *right* read *left*.
2 Use a mirror to reverse diagrams.
3 Sit opposite a friend and copy the movements reversing them at the same time.

It is also possible for some left-handed workers to learn to crochet in the usual right-handed way by holding the hook fairly stationary and placing the yarn round the hook by moving the left hand. The left hand does all the work. This is a very useful method for people with impaired movement of the right hand.

Whichever method you choose, it is important that you are consistent. Become accustomed to examining your work and understand what you are doing. If you have made a mistake it does not matter as long as you know why you went wrong and how to put it right. The way you hold your work and how and where you put the hook will influence the finished result. It is important to do things always in exactly the same way or your work will look uneven and the tension will be poor. Crochet is a very individual craft and even with identical teaching it is seldom that any two people hold their yarn and work exactly the same way. In the countries bordering on the Mediterranean crocheters hold their hooks facing the body but we tend to hold our hooks away from the body. This does not matter as long as the finished result is even and pleasing.

Working in the Round

Our grandmothers always taught crochet in the round and many tears were shed over circles which would not lay flat. It is difficult to judge how much increasing is necessary to keep the work flat. A foundation chain is necessary which is joined with a slip stitch (sl st).

Round 1 Make 6ch, place hook through 1st st and pull yarn through and through 2nd lp on hook. This is a slip stitch. (A slip stitch is a joining stitch or one for travelling along the work. It has no depth, only the thickness of the yarn.) Make 3tch and work 2tr into 2nd st. (This is increasing [inc].) Work 2tr into every st to end of round and 1tr into last st. Sl st to top of tch to close up round, 3ch. This will give a circle of 12st including the tch as the 1st st. Do not turn.

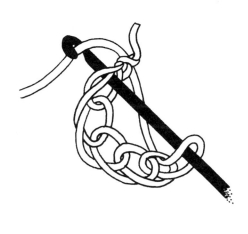

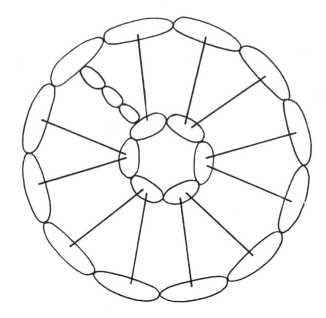

Fig 23

Round 2 2tr into 2nd st and 2tr into every following st finishing with 1tr into last st. Sl st to top of tch, 3ch (24st).
Round 3 Repeat Round 2 which will result in 48st. The tch counts as 1st.

If these instructions are worked in chunky yarn with a 7.00mm hook they will make the crown of a hat. Continue working straight with no further increases until the hat is as deep as you like it, then add a brim in a contrasting yarn.

To make a much larger circle, more increases are necessary. Increase every other stitch for one round and then every two or three stitches on following rounds. It is impossible to give accurate instructions because the type of yarn and size of hook influence the result (see beret Design 7, page 99).

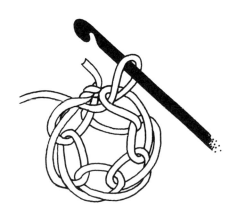

Fig 22

If textured yarn such as mohair or bouclé is used, you will find that the texture tends to be at the back of the work. This is because the work is not turned at the end of the round. To correct this, turn the work every round after making the three chain. Alternatively it is often a good idea to take advantage of the texture and use the back as the right side. For instance, the fluffiness of mohair can be brushed up much more if the wrong side is used. In crochet the so-called wrong side sometimes looks more attractive than what is meant to be the right side. There are no rules, just use whichever you like best. Working in the round can be used to save seams and sleeves, and skirts, socks, etc can be made from tubular shapes. When crocheting in this way it is most important to turn the work at the end of every round after the turning chain. Failure to do this will result in a slightly warped effect.

Simple Projects

It is a good idea to make things as soon as you can work a treble crochet, keep the work even and the edges straight. The practice obtained by making very small easy items gives confidence to tackle more difficult things.

Remember that, at this stage, you have only mastered a chain and a treble and there is still much to learn. Take out all your odd wools and try any of the following, all made from squares and rectangles.

1   A shopping bag.
2   A tote bag with crochet handle.
3   A work bag with plastic handles sewn on.
4   A belt with buckle or ties.
5   A scarf crocheted from side to side.
6   A scarf made with a basic chain as long as you wish the scarf to be.
7   An evening stole with fringe.
8   A tabard from two rectangles (see Design 3, page 92).
9   An evening bag – a rectangle folded into three (see Design 2, page 91).
10   A suntop from two rectangles.

The list is endless and no doubt you will be able to think of many more. Use odd wools for stripes and join various textures and thicknesses together. Always use inexpensive yarn until you are really satisfied with your work. When your tension is good, then is the time to be adventurous. Mix and match your yarns; use textures such as bouclé; twist and mix different types and colours of yarn together; experiment with string, macramé thread and ribbon for belts and bags. Add embroidery and beads to your trebles. Buy odd cheap yarns from the bins in wool shops or beg left-over yarn from friends. Tie fairly short pieces of yarn of varying textures together and then crochet for an interesting result.

When you feel confident enough to embark on a garment, only buy one ball of your chosen yarn at first. Try the stitch with the yarn and different hooks to make sure you like the effect you are getting. When you are quite happy with the fabric made from the combination of stitch and yarn, then buy enough for the garment. Make sure that all the yarn you buy is from the same dye lot. It is very difficult to estimate how much yarn you need but good wool shops will give you an idea and they will usually exchange unused balls. You should now be able to make the projects in Designs 1–5, pages 90–97.

Fig 24   Ideas from rectangles

Lesson 2
INCREASING YOUR SKILLS

Crochet Stitches

You should now be quite familiar with holding the hook and yarn and how to crochet using only the treble stitch. Possibly several projects have been completed successfully, you will have developed confidence and ideas are beginning to flow. Crochet is rather like learning to play the piano. daily practice helps tremendously. The rest of the stitches will now be learned very quickly and easily.

To form a base for the following stitches, make a strip of chain and work on it about 20 trebles. It is easier to work into a stitch rather than into a chain. Always work from right to left.

Slip Stitch (sl st)
1 Insert hook into 2nd st next to hook.
2 yrh.
3 Pull lp through st and through lp on hook at the same time. (This st has no depth and so requires no tch.)

Double Crochet (dc)
1 1tch.
2 Insert hook into 2nd st.
3 yrh.
4 Pull thread through. 2lps on hook.
5 yrh and pull through the 2lps.
6 Repeat into next st.

Fig 26

Fig 25

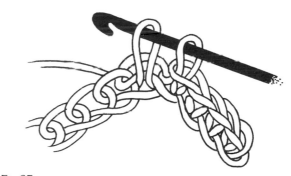

Fig 27

Slip stitch is used for joining chains into a circle (see Lesson 1, page 20) or for travelling along the work when decreasing a number of stitches together, for example for an armhole.

Double crochet is used for edgings. It makes a firm tight fabric but it is not often used for garments on its own. It is usually part of a stitch pattern. Try working the stitch but always inserting the hook into the back loop of the stitch. This makes a very satisfactory crochet rib but it is worked sideways and has to be sewn or crocheted on to the garment or, alternatively, work the ribbing, turn it sideways and crochet along the ends of the rows (see Design 10, page 103 and Design 14, page 110).

Half Treble (htr)
Make 2tch.
1   yrh.
2   Insert hook into 2nd st.
3   yrh and pull through 1lp. 3lps on hook.
4   yrh and pull through 3lps.
Continue working into every stitch.

This makes a firm thicker stitch suitable for jackets.

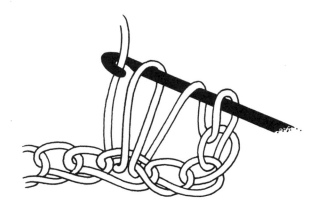

Fig 28

Fig 29

Treble (tr)
For those following the course this stitch may be skipped as it has already been fully covered in Lesson 1.
Make 3tch.
1   yrh.
2   Insert hook into 2nd st.
3   yrh and pull through. 3lps on hook.
4   yrh and pull through 2lps.
5   yrh and pull through last 2lps on hook.
Repeat into every stitch.

This stitch is probably used more than any of the others.

Double Treble (dtr)
Make 4tch.
1   yrh twice.
2   Insert hook into 2nd st.
3   yrh and pull through. 4lps on hook.
4   yrh and pull through 2lps. 3lps on hook.
5   Repeat step 4. 2lps on hook.
6   Repeat step 4.

This is a taller stitch and is used for lacy patterns and textured crochet.

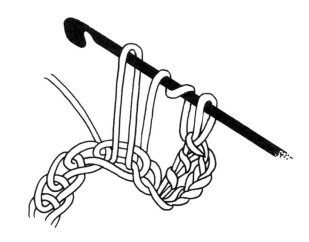

Fig 30

Triple Treble (tr tr)

Make 5tch.
1 yrh three times.
2 Insert hook into 2nd st.
3 yrh and pull through. 5lps on hook.
4 yrh and pull through 2lps. 4lps on hook.
5 Repeat step 4 three times until 1lp remains on hook.

It is possible to continue making trebles as long as you like by putting the yarn round the hook more times but this is just common sense and does not need further explanation. A triple treble would make a satisfactory belt loop.

Fig.31

Turning Chain (tch)

Turning chain is the chain at the end of the row to accommodate the height of the stitch. Some commercial patterns give this at the beginning of the row and others at the end. To obtain a firm straight edge to your work count the turning chain as the first stitch.

Consequently, when the work is turned, it makes the last stitch of the previous row and so a stitch must always be worked into it. This is not always easy but to make a firm edge a stitch should be worked into the turning chain rather than the space between the turning chain and the last stitch. Sometimes when working trebles there is a small hole at the end of every other row. This is because the turning chain is loose, perhaps through thick yarn or a slack tension. To correct this use two turning chain instead of three at the end of the row. Some patterns give two turning chain for trebles and some will give three. Experience will help you to find out whether your tension needs two or three stitches.

Turning chain	Number of chain
Slip stitch (sl st)	0
Double crochet (dc)	1
Half treble (htr)	2
Treble (tr)	2 or 3
Double treble (dtr)	4
Triple treble (ttr)	5
Quadruple treble (quad tr)	6 and so on

The work can be kept straight and even at the edges whatever the stitch by keeping to the principle learned in Lesson 1 of missing the first stitch at the beginning of the row and working a stitch into the turning chain at the end of the row. This is for plain crochet instructions in one stitch only. The instructions for complicated patterns will be self-explanatory.

Increasing (inc)

Gradual Increasing to Make a Curve

Work two stitches into one space. The turning chain counts as the first stitch so the increase has to be on the second stitch. At the end of the row increase by working two stitches into one space on the last stitch but one.

At the end of the row Attach a spare piece of yarn to the previous row and work a number of chain. Crochet across the row and use the spare chain at the end to make the number of stitches you wish to increase. Unpick the spare chain not required.

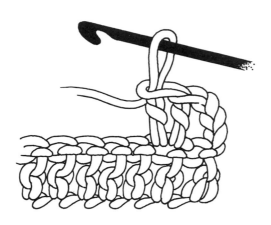

Fig 32

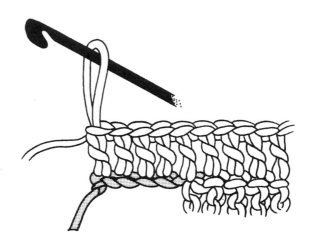

Fig 34

Increasing a Number of Stitches at Once

At the beginning of the row Deduct one from the number of stitches you wish to add in chains plus the number of turning chain for the stitch being used. For example, if the stitch being used was treble and five more stitches were needed, then 4+3tch=7ch. Seven chain would give an increase of five trebles.

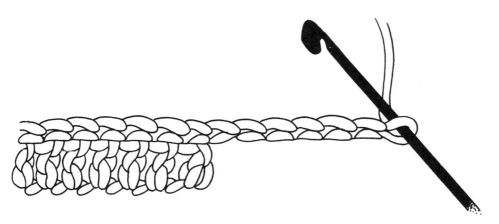

Fig 33

Decreasing (dec)

Gradual Decreasing to Make a Curve

It is possible just to miss a stich but often this is not very satisfactory as it makes a hole. The best way to decrease is to work whatever stitch you are using until there are two loops left on the hook, then work the next stitch to the same stage so there will be three loops on the hook. Yarn round hook and work the three loops together. Work in this manner at the beginning of the row after the turning chain and on the second and third stitch before the last stitch at the end of the row.

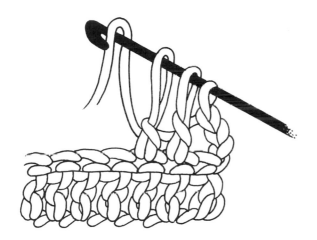

Fig 35

Decreasing a Number of Stiches at Once

At the beginning of the row Use a slip stitch to travel along the work the number of necessary stitches, take one more slip stitch and work the standing chain. Check that you have decreased the required number.

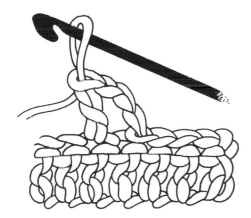

Fig 36

At the end of the row Crochet along the row and leave the required number of stitches unworked. Make the turning chain for the next row and turn.

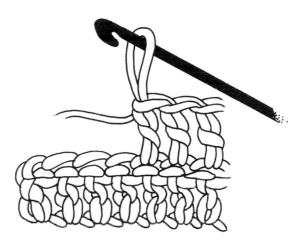

Fig 37

Understanding Commercial Patterns

Many people say 'I can crochet but can't read a pattern.' If they were honest they would admit that they had never seriously applied themselves to reading a pattern or that they did not like following instructions. Beginners who are following this book will find that instructions are beginning to make sense because they are becoming familiar with the abbreviations.

Commercial Patterns are written under the following headings:

Materials

Details of quantity of yarn, hooks needed and buttons or any other accessories needed to complete the garment.

Tension

The number of stitches or rows to 10cm (4in).

Sizes

Pattern instructions are usually in two, three or four sizes with larger sizes in brackets.

Abbreviations

All the most usual abbreviations for the stitches and for working the pattern are given, including any individual abbreviations for groups of stitches peculiar to that particular design. For example, *blk* for a block of stitches or *gr* for a group.

Instructions

Details necessary to make all the separate parts of the project in the particular stitch. It is helpful if there are diagrams with measurements of each individual piece needed for the garment.

Sewing up and finishing off

Details of how to assemble the garment including any edging or finishing details.

Many people buy the correct yarn and hooks and, ignoring everything else, start straight away on the instructions of 150 chain or whatever. This is a recipe for disappointment and disaster.

How to Read a Pattern

1   Read right through *all* the instructions leaving out the actual stitch instructions.
2   Make sure that you are completely familiar with the design.
3   Study the abbreviations and make sure you know what they all mean.
4   Try the stitch instructions. If you find them difficult work one stitch at a time. A friend reading the instructions to you one stitch at a time is often a help. Do exactly what the pattern instructions say – not what you think they say. There is often quite a difference!

Crochet instructions are often very difficult to write. It is not easy to explain all the movements which, in themselves, are easy to do but often difficult to put in writing, so you need to follow the instructions slowly and carefully. Here are some examples:

Into the first chain means the first chain worked and not the chain next to the hook.

Into a st means into the top of the stitch making two loops of the stitch on the hook.

Into a sp means into the space between the bars of the stitches.

Into a 2ch sp means into the space under the two chain. The loop on the hook does not count as a stitch.

For a full list of abbreviations see page 9. Notice that the American abbreviations are different but some books and continental magazines do use American terms.

International Symbols

These are used on the continent and in Japan. They are very useful because the pattern is explained in a diagrammatic or graph form and language is not necessary. Unfortunately they are not popular in this country.

Tension

This part of the pattern is usually ignored but it is ESSENTIAL if garments are to turn out the right size. Tension in knitting is much easier to cope with than tension in crochet. Knitters usually know if their tension is tight or loose and they alter the needle size accordingly.

Tension in crochet is much more difficult. Crochet is such an individual craft that the tension of the pattern is peculiar only to the designer. Your tension can vary from week to week and can even vary with how you are feeling physically and mentally. Crochet garments should always be finished and not put away to be completed later because a looser or tighter tension might make a tremendous difference.

How to Work a Tension Square

This is usually ignored but checking the tension is vital to the success of the garment and failure to do this is often the reason for failures with crochet.

1   With the correct yarn and hook make a chain about 20cm (8in) long. Follow the stitch instructions and where the pattern says repeat from * to the end of the row, repeat as many times as your chain will allow. Follow the instructions until you have a square of about 20cm (8in).
2   Cut a piece of cardboard with a window of 10cm (4in) square.
3   Place the square in the centre of the stitch sample and count the number of stitches across the top of the square and the number of rows down the square. Compare this with the details given in the tension section of the pattern.

It is essential to get the number of stitches correct first because the rows are easily adjusted by doing more or less. If there are too many stitches in your sample, try a larger hook. If there are not enough stitches you need a smaller hook. One stitch out in 10cm (4in) could mean anything up to 10cm (4in) difference in the finished width of the garment, so you must get it right before you start.

Garment Sizes

Instructions for two, three or four sizes are usually given with the smallest size first and the larger sizes in brackets. Before starting, circle with a coloured pencil throughout the pattern the size you intend to make.

Tension for Your Own Design

If you are going to make your own design you will want to know how many stitches to use. Make a tension square and count the number of stitches in 10cm (4in), divide by 10 (4) and multiply by the bust or chest measurement you need and this will give the number of stitches for all round the garment. Use the following table as a guide.

Stitches in	Chest or bust measurement											
4 in / 10 cm	22 in / 56 cm	24 in / 61 cm	26 in / 66 cm	28 in / 71 cm	30 in / 76 cm	32 in / 81 cm	34 in / 86 cm	36 in / 91 cm	38 in / 96 cm	40 in / 102 cm	42 in / 107 cm	44 in / 112 cm
10	56	61	66	71	76	81	86	91	96	102	107	112
11	62	67	73	78	82	89	95	100	106	112	118	123
12	67	73	79	85	89	97	103	109	115	123	129	135
13	73	79	86	93	96	106	112	119	125	133	139	146
14	79	86	95	100	107	114	121	128	135	143	150	157
15	84	92	99	107	114	122	129	137	144	153	161	168
16	89	98	106	114	122	130	138	146	154	164	172	180
17	95	104	112	121	130	138	147	155	164	174	182	191
18	101	110	119	128	137	146	155	164	173	184	193	202
19	107	116	125	135	145	154	164	173	183	194	204	213
20	112	122	132	142	152	162	172	182	192	204	214	224
21	118	128	139	149	160	171	181	192	202	215	225	236
22	123	134	145	156	168	179	190	201	212	224	236	247
23	129	140	152	163	175	187	198	210	221	235	247	258
24	135	145	159	171	183	195	207	219	231	245	257	269
25	140	153	165	178	190	203	215	228	240	255	268	280
26	146	159	172	185	198	211	224	237	250	266	279	292
27	151	165	178	192	206	219	233	246	260	276	289	303
28	157	171	185	199	213	227	241	255	269	286	300	314
29	162	177	192	206	221	235	250	264	279	296	311	325
30	168	183	198	213	228	244	258	273	288	306	321	336

This table can be used for knitting as well as crochet.
1   Make a tension square with the yarn and hook or needles to be used for the garment.
2   Count the number of stitches over 10cm (4in).
3   Find the number in the first column.
4   Move the finger across the square until it is under the required size. This is the number you need if the garment is to be made in one piece.
5   For separate backs and fronts divide by two.
6   For one front divide by four.

Note that the number of stitches is a guide and adjustments will be necessary to balance fancy stitch patterns.

Fancy Stitch Patterns

For practice in reading patterns try some of the following stitch patterns.

Arch Stitch
Make 20ch.
Row 1 1dc into 8th ch, *5ch, miss 3st, 1dc*. Repeat from * to end of row, 5ch, turn.
Row 2 1dc into centre ch of 5ch lp of previous row, *5ch, 1dc into 3rd ch of 5ch sp. Repeat from * to end of row, 5ch, turn.
Row 2 forms pattern

Openwork Checks
Make 14ch.
Row 1 3ch, *1tr in each of next 4ch, 1ch, miss 1ch*. Finish row with 4tr.
Row 2 *4ch, insert hook into 1ch sp 1dc*. Repeat from * to end of row working last dc into tch, 3ch, turn.
Row 3 Crochet groups of *4tr into each 4ch sp, 1ch miss 1st*. Repeat from * to end of row finishing with 4tr.
Rows 2 and 3 form pattern

Clusters
Make 12ch.
Row 1 2ch* (yrh, insert hook into 4th ch from hook, draw through a lp, yrh draw through 2lps on hook) 3 times into same st, yrh, draw through 8lps on hook, 1ch, miss 1ch. Repeat from * to end of row finishing with 1 cluster, 2ch, turn.
Row 2 Work clusters into 1ch spaces with 1ch between, 2ch, turn.
Row 2 forms pattern

Bodkin Stitch
Make 25ch.
Row 1 1tr into 4th ch, 1tr, *miss 3st (2tr 2ch 2tr) into next st, miss 3st, 3tr. Repeat from * to end of ch, 2ch, turn.
Row 2 2tr *miss 3st (2tr 2ch 2tr) into 2ch sp, miss 3st, 3tr. Repeat from * to end of row, 2ch, turn.
Row 2 forms pattern

Lesson 3

DESIGN WITH COLOUR, SHAPE AND TEXTURE

Many people think that designing is for the artist and out of the question for them, but this is not so. It is much easier to make a paper shape or pattern and crochet a fabric to fit the shape than it is to read commercial patterns which have so many limitations. It is best to start with the easiest shape – a rectangle – and progress from there.

Measurements needed:
1 Length of garment – hip, waist or full length.
2 Length of sleeve from underarm – short, threequarter or long.

3 Bust or chest measurement – crochet fabric does not need as much allowance for ease as a woven fabric. Measure round the bust fairly loosely. If a large loose garment is required, add inches accordingly or measure garments already in use.

Shape No 1

A Tabard or Over-jumper
This can be made to fit all sizes from a small child to a large lady. The size of armhole and length of shoulder seam will vary in length with the size of the garment.

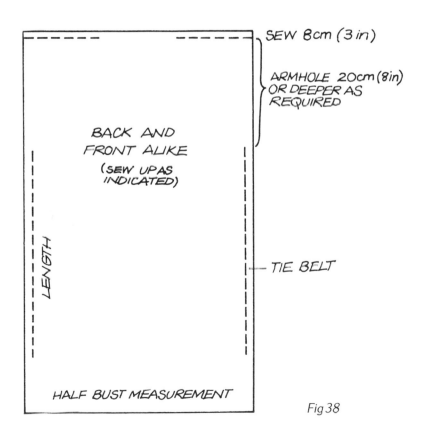

Fig 38

Variations on the Tabard

If you are confident, an expensive, attractive yarn will give an exclusive garment. A bouclé yarn is difficult to use because you cannot see the stitches but it covers up an uneven tension and camouflages any mistakes.

Fig 39

Fig 40

Fig 41

Fig 42

Fig 43

Fig 44

A Jacket from Rectangles

Crochet the pattern pieces in the yarn and stitch of your choice. You can work in any direction you like – from the bottom hem upwards or sideways from the centre back to the side seam, rejoining the yarn at the centre back and working out to the other side. It is even possible to work diagonally across in stripes but this is not recommended for beginners. As long as your crochet fabric matches the pattern pieces in size, the garment will fit. Neaten all the edges with one row of treble or one row of double crochet. This can be in a contrasting colour. Suggestions for edgings are given in Lesson 6.

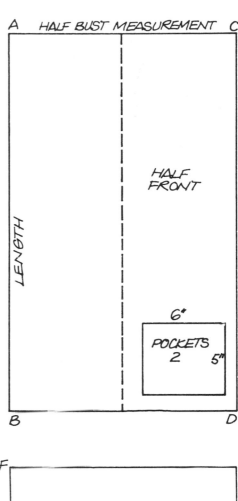

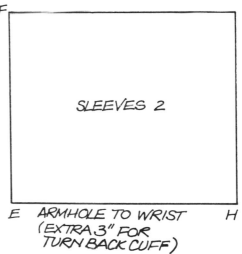

Fig 46

Fig 45

Shape No 2

Basic Shape for Jackets, Waistcoats and Coats

Make this basic shape to your size. It can be used to check the size of commercial patterns you may follow or it can be used as the base of your own designs.

1   Take a large rectangular sheet of paper.
2   Mark off your bust measurement along one side and the length you like your jackets along the other side. Cut to size.
3   Fold in halves along the dotted line making the centre back position (Fig 47).
4   Fold in halves again making four sections. The new folds give the underarm seam position. The two edges are the centre fronts (Fig 48).
5   Cut along the side with the two folds down 20cm (8in) and 3cm (1½in). This makes the two armholes.

6   Open out (Fig 49) and refold into jacket shape (Fig 50).
7   In sizes larger than 102cm (40in) bust it will be necessary to have the armhole deeper and a little wider and for smaller sizes the armhole will be shorter and correspondingly narrower.
8   The top of the back is divided into thirds making one third for the neck edge and one third for each shoulder.
9   The front shoulder measurement can be obtained by placing along the back shoulder and folding back revers as in Fig 45.
10   Cut the sleeve pattern (see Fig 46). Add 7.5cm (3in) extra for turn-back cuff.

This pattern makes a garment with a slightly dropped shoulder line and a wide sleeve.

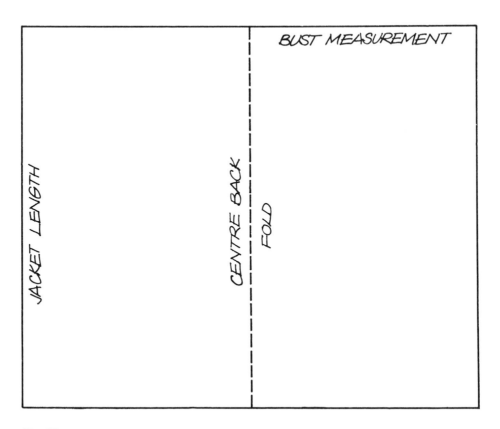

Fig 47

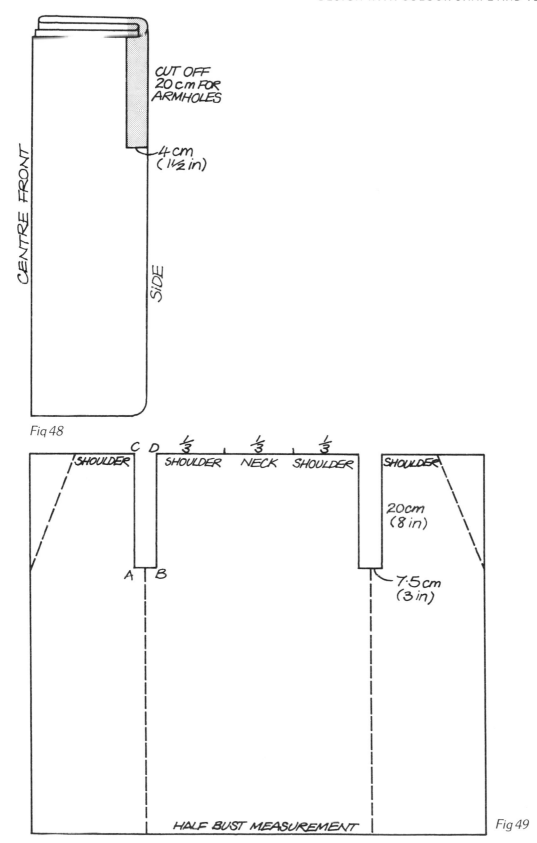

CENTRE FRONT

CUT OFF
20 cm FOR
ARMHOLES

4 cm
(1½ in)

SIDE

Fig 48

SHOULDER   C D   ⅓   ⅓   ⅓

SHOULDER   NECK   SHOULDER   SHOULDER

20cm
(8 in)

A B

7·5cm
(3 in)

HALF BUST MEASUREMENT   *Fig 49*

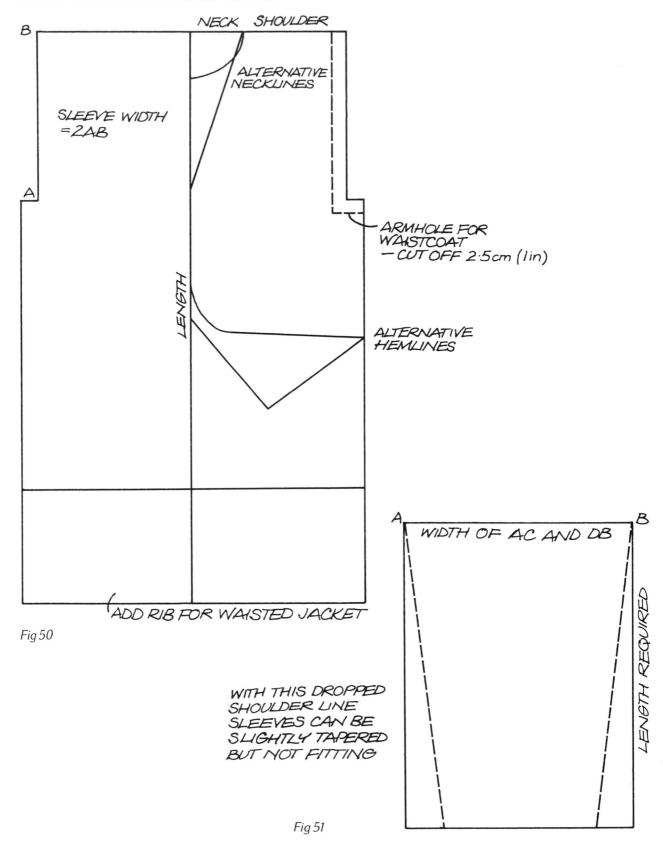

B

SLEEVE WIDTH
=2AB

A

NECK   SHOULDER

ALTERNATIVE
NECKLINES

ARMHOLE FOR
WAISTCOAT
— CUT OFF 2·5cm (1in)

LENGTH

ALTERNATIVE
HEMLINES

ADD RIB FOR WAISTED JACKET

Fig 50

WITH THIS DROPPED
SHOULDER LINE
SLEEVES CAN BE
SLIGHTLY TAPERED
BUT NOT FITTING

Fig 51

A   WIDTH OF AC AND DB   B

LENGTH REQUIRED

Converting Pattern to a Fitted Top

1   Use either a dressmaking pattern of the size you want or an unpicked garment which fits.

2   Trim any seam allowances.

3   Place pattern over basic shape and re-draw the shoulder, armholes and neckline. Use fitted sleeve of dressmaking pattern because a shaped armhole must have a shaped sleeve head.

Any dressmaking pattern which is cut for knitted fabrics can be used as a shape for making a crochet fabric. Place the crochet on to the pattern and increase or decrease as necessary to make the garment shape, the same shape as the pattern with seam allowance removed.

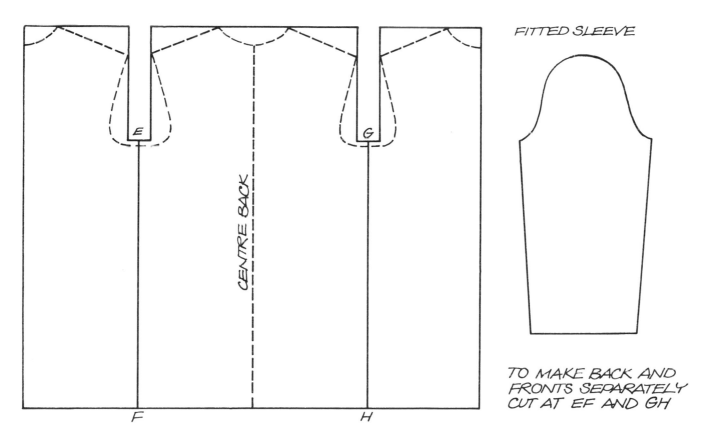

FITTED SLEEVE

TO MAKE BACK AND FRONTS SEPARATELY CUT AT EF AND GH

Fig 52

(opposite) A variety of stitch samples to inspire your own ideas.

(top left) White mohair woven with double thickness of blue rainbow-dyed bouclé.
Make a tricot mesh by working 1tr 1ch for every row in white.
Weave the bouclé or a contrasting yarn in and out using an ordinary darning weave.

(centre left) Broomstick stitch in lurex and mohair.
Use a 25mm (1in) broomstick and a 6mm hook.
Make an even number of ch. Slip the last lp on to the broomstick.
Hold the broomstick under the left arm.
Insert the hook into every ch and pull up a lp and place on the broomstick.
To remove the stitches
Row 1 Insert the hook into the first 2 lps and make 1ch to hold them together. Work 2dc into the lps. Continue removing 2 lps with 2dc to the end of the row. Place the last lp on to the broomstick.
Row 2 Insert the hook into the back lp of the dc and pull up a lp. Continue all along the row.
These 2 rows form the pattern.

(bottom left) Rust and green Tunisian crochet design on stone background (looked at upside down, this design resembles rows of flowers).
Make a number of ch divisible by 4 plus 3.
Row 1 Using colour A (stone) 3tch, work 1 row of Ttr.
Row 2 Return row of Ttr.
Row 3 Tdc.
Row 4 Tunisian return row.
Row 5 3Tdc. Attach colour B (rust) *1 bobble st, 3Tdc in colour A. Repeat from * to end of row.
Row 6 Colour A, Tunisian return row.
Row 7 3Tdc. *Attach colour C (green). Make 1Ttr tr into row 3 2st back, leave the last lp on the hook, 1dc into the st, 1Ttr tr into row 3 2st forward, yrh and work the 3lps together. 3Tdc in colour A. Repeat from * to end of row.
Row 8 Tunisian return row.
Row 9 Ttr.
Row 10 Tunisian return row.
Row 11 1Tdc, *work 1 bobble st in colour B, 3Tdc in colour A. Repeat from * to end of row finishing with 1Tdc.
Row 12 Tunisian return row.
Row 13 1Tdc. Attach colour C and work as in row 7.
Row 14 Tunisian return row.
Row 15 Ttr.
Row 16 Tunisian return row.

(top right) Basket stitch raised trebles in 3 colours.
Work an even number of ch in colour A.
Row 1 3tch, tr into every ch.
Row 2 1RtrF, *2RtrB, 2RtrF. Repeat from * to end of row. 2ch, turn.
Work 2 rows of each colour and alternate the stitches every 2 rows to obtain the basket effect.

(centre right – upper) Brick pattern – grey background with rainbow-dyed mohair yarn as contrast – Tunisian crochet.
Using colour A, make a number of ch divisible by 4 plus 3.

Row 1 Tdc.
Row 2 Tunisian return row.
Row 3 Colour B, Tdc.
Row 4 Tunisian return row.
Row 5 Colour A, as row 1.
Row 6 As row 2.
Rows 7 and 8 Repeat rows 1 and 2.
Row 9 Colour B, 2Tdc, *1Ttr tr into row 3, 3Tdc. Repeat from * to end of row.
Row 10 Tunisian return row.
Rows 11 to 14 Colour A, repeat rows 5 to 8.
Row 15 Colour B, 4Tdc, *1Ttr tr into row 9, 3Tdc. Repeat from * to end of row.
Row 16 Tunisian return row.
Continue working in this pattern which will give a brick effect.

(centre right – lower) Cream chunky mohair with rainbow bouclé contrast – Tunisian crochet.
Using colour A, make a number of ch divisible by 4 plus 3.
Row 1 Tdc.
Row 2 Tunisian return row.
Rows 3 and 4 Repeat rows 1 and 2.
Row 5 Colour B, 1Ttr working into previous row, *2Tp, 2Ttr into previous row. Repeat from * to end of row.
Row 6 Tunisian return row.
Rows 7 to 10 Colour A, repeat rows 1 to 4.
Row 11 Colour B, 1Tp, *2Ttr into previous row, 2Tp. Repeat from * to end of row.
Row 12 Tunisian return row.
Rows 5 to 12 form the pattern.

(bottom right) Brown chunky mohair with gold spots – Tunisian crochet.
Using colour A (brown), make a number of ch divisible by 6.
Row 1 Tdc.
Row 2 Tunisian return row.
Row 3 As row 1.
Row 4 As row 2.
Row 5 2Tdc. Attach colour B (gold) *1 bobble st, 5Tdc in colour A. Repeat from * to end of row.
Row 6 Tunisian return row.
Rows 7 and 8 As rows 1 and 2.
Row 9 5Tdc. Attach colour B *1 bobble st, 5Tdc in colour A. Repeat from * to end of row.
Row 10 Tunisian return row.
These 10 rows form the pattern.

(overleaf left)
Design 13: Batwing Jumper and Matching Hat (page 108)

(overleaf right)
Design 9: Summer Cardigan and Suntop in Cotton (page 101)

40

The stitch samples on this page are all worked in Tunisian crochet. Very simple Tunisian stitches are used and the variety of textures is obtained by using yarns of different colours and textures. The woven look is obtained by changing the yarn on the left at the beginning of the return row, and the yarn is usually changed every 2 rows, though in some cases every row. This means that using yarns of different thicknesses does not matter as – provided a very thick yarn is followed by a much thinner one – they will compensate for each other and all will be well! Any of these samples can be attempted after working through Lesson 5.

(top left – 7 colours)
Row 1 Colour A, Tdc.
Row 2 Colour B, Tunisian return row.
Row 3 Colour B, Ttr.
Row 4 Colour C, Tunisian return row.
Row 5 Colour C, 1Tdc, 1Tdtr into the st in row 1.
Row 6 Colour D, Tunisian return row.
Row 7 Colour D, Tp.
Row 8 Colour E, Tunisian return row.
Row 9 Colour E, Tdc.
Row 10 Colour D, Tunisian return row.
Row 11 Colour F, Ttr.
Row 12 Colour F, Tunisian return row.
Row 13 Colour F, *1 bobble st, 3Tdc. Repeat from * to end of row.
Row 14 Colour G, Tunisian return row.
Row 15 Colour G, *1Tdc, 1Tp. Repeat from * to end of row.
Row 16 Colour E, Tunisian return row.
Row 17 Colour E, Tdc.
Row 18 Colour E, Tunisian return row.

(centre left – 7 colours)
Row 1 Colour A, Tdc.
Row 2 Colour B, Tunisian return row.
Row 3 Colour C, Tp.
Row 4 Colour D, Tunisian return row.
Row 5 Colour D, Tp.
Row 6 Colour E, Tunisian return row.
Row 7 Colour E, Tp.
Row 8 Colour A, Tunisian return row.
Row 9 Colour F, Ttr.
Row 10 Colour G, Tunisian return row.
Row 11 Colour G, Tdc.
Row 12 Colour G, Tunisian return row.

(bottom left – 7 colours)
Row 1 Colour A, Ttr.
Row 2 Colour B, Tunisian return row.
Row 3 Colour B, Ttr.
Row 4 Colour C, Tunisian return row.
Row 5 Colour C, *1Tdc, 1Ttr dropped into lp of row 1. Repeat from * to end of row.
Row 6 Colour D, Tunisian return row.
Row 7 Colour D, Tp.
Row 8 Colour E, Tunisian return row.

Row 9 Colour E, Tdc.
Row 10 Colour A, Tunisian return row.
Row 11 Colour A, Tp.
Row 12 Colour E, Tunisian return row.
Row 13 Colour E, Ttr.
Row 14 Colour D, Tunisian return row.
Row 15 Colour D, *4Tdc, 1Ttr tr into the previous row 2st to the right, 1Tdc, 1Ttr tr into the previous row 2st to the left, yrh and pull through 3lps. Repeat from * to end of row.
Row 16 Colour F, Tunisian return row.
Row 17 Colour F, *4Tdc, 1 bobble st. Repeat from * to end of row.
Row 18 Colour G, Tunisian return row.
Row 19 Colour G, Ttr.
Row 20 Colour A, Tunisian return row.

(top right – 5 colours)
Row 1 Colour A, Ttr.
Row 2 Colour B, Tunisian return row.
Row 3 Colour B, Tp.
Row 4 Colour C, Tunisian return row.
Row 5 Colour C, Tdc.
Row 6 Colour D, Tunisian return row.
Row 7 Colour D, Ttr.
Row 8 Colour C, Tunisian return row.
Row 9 Colour C, *2Tp, 1 bobble st. Repeat from * to end of row.
Row 10 Colour D, Tunisian return row.
Row 11 Colour D, Ttr.
Row 12 Colour C, Tunisian return row.
Row 13 Colour C, Tdc.
Row 14 Colour A, Tunisian return row.
Row 15 Colour A, Ttr.
Row 16 Colour B, Tunisian return row.
Row 17 Colour B, Tp.
Row 18 Colour A, Tunisian return row.

(centre right – 2 colours)
Row 1 Colour A, Ttr.
Row 2 Colour B, Tunisian return row.
Row 3 Colour B, Tdc.
Row 4 Colour A, Tunisian return row.
These 4 rows form the pattern.

(bottom right – 6 colours)
Row 1 Colour A, Ttr.
Row 2 Colour B, Tunisian return row.
Row 3 Colour C, *1Tdc, 1Tp. Repeat from * to end of row.
Row 4 Colour A, Tunisian return row.
Row 5 Colour A, Ttr.
Row 6 Colour D, Tunisian return row.
Row 7 Colour D, Tp.
Row 8 Colour A, Tunisian return row.
Row 9 Colour A, Ttr.
Row 10 Colour E, Tunisian return row.
Row 11 Colour E, Tp.
Row 12 Colour F, Tunisian return row.
Row 13 Colour F, Tdc.
Row 14 Colour A, Tunisian return row.

Converting Pattern to a Coat

(see Design 20, page 121)

1　Cut pattern along side-seam position.
2　Add 3cm (1in) at hip line (see Fig 53).
3　Extend to length required.
4　Re-draw the side seam.

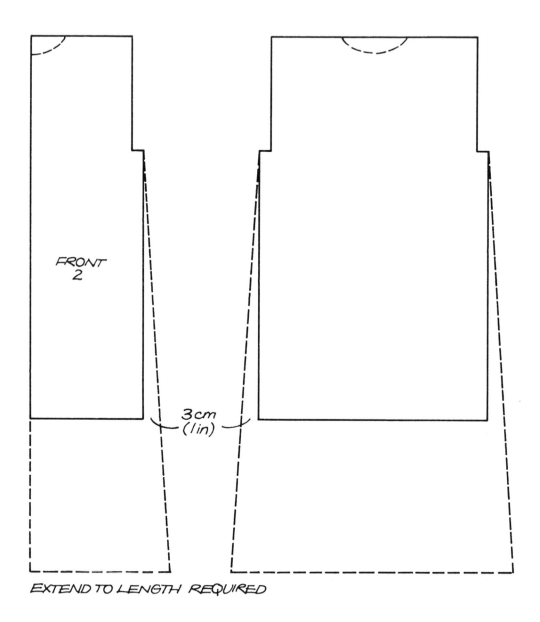

FRONT
2

3cm
(1in)

EXTEND TO LENGTH REQUIRED

Fig 53

Shape No 3

The Batwing

Measurements needed:
Shoulder to waist – multiply by 2 (EGGF)
Waist measurement – divide by 4 (EA or FC)
Sleeve measurement taken from neck to wrist (GH)

To Make Up

1   Crochet sideways from EF to BC. This makes half back, half front and one sleeve.
2   Crochet second side to match.

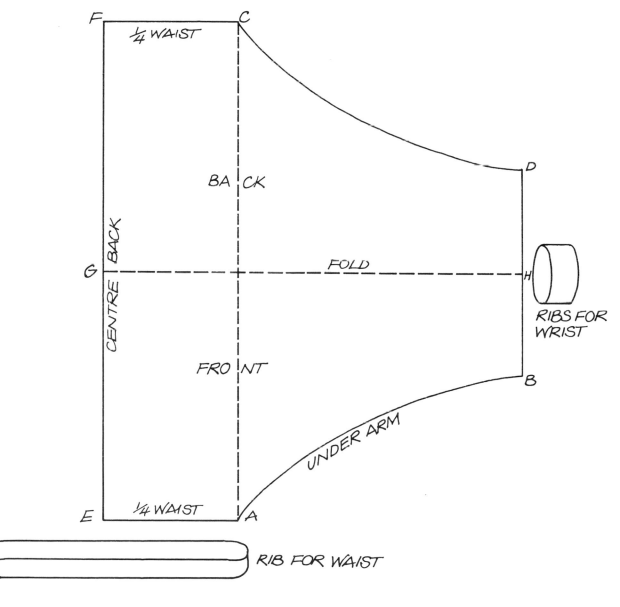

Fig 54

3   Crochet edgings along the two centre-front and back edges E to F.

4   If a jacket is required, make buttonholes on right front edge.

5   Sew underarm seams AB to CD.

6   Sew sleeve ribs to the end of sleeves or continue sleeves with crochet.

7   Sew centre back to within 13cm (5in) of G.

8   Sew centre front leaving neck opening for jumper.

9   Sew side seams AB to CD.

10   Sew ribbing to bottom of jumper or jacket or pick up stitches at the bottom and crochet the rib.

For Smaller Sleeves and Fitted Neckline

Make new sleeve line from A to B and C to D to give a more fitted sleeve. Shape neckline to make a more fitted garment. For this shape there must be a neck opening.

Fig 56

Fig 55

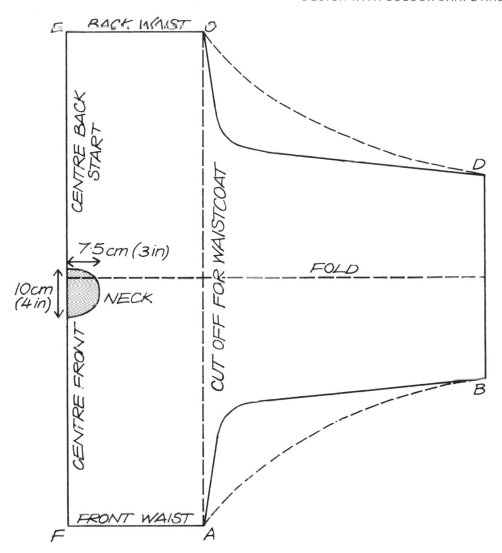

Fig 57   Adaptation of shape for jacket with smaller
sleeves and a fitted round neckline

To Crochet from Centre Back to Wrist
(see Design 14, page 110)
1   Start at centre back and work to edge of neck
shaping. Put to one side.
2   Start again at centre front and work to neck edge.
3   Increase along neck edge of front to make back and
front the same length.
4   Continue working across front and back together, to
the bottom of the sleeve.
5   Pick up stitches along centre back and work in the
same way to the bottom of the other sleeve.

A Waistcoat from Shape 3

1   Make two strips the size of FA, EC.
2   Fold each strip in half and sew along one side leaving 20cm (8in) for the armhole.
3   Add edgings and ribs as for jacket.

This shape, although unusual, makes an attractive waistcoat (see Broomstick Crochet Waistcoat, Design 18, page 118).

Figs 59–62 show collars, necklines, sleeves and pockets to use with the basic garment shapes.

ADAPTATION FROM SHAPE NO 3

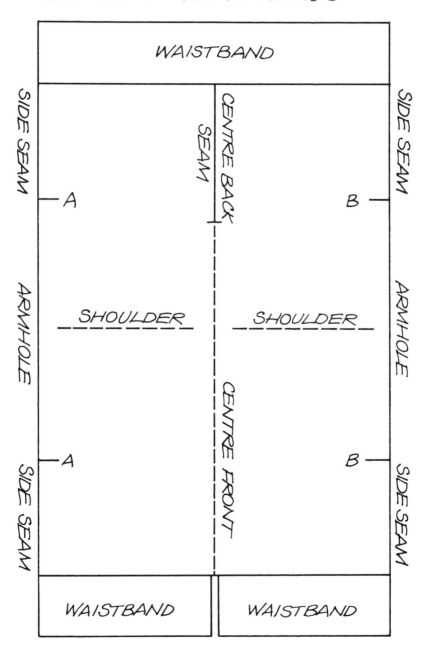

Fig 58

COLLARS

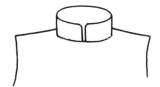

MANDARIN ~ PICK
UP NECKLINE
AND CROCHET EDGE

POLO ~ STRAIGHT
RIB SEWN UP

TURN BACK COLLAR
~ STRAIGHT STRIP OF
RIBBED CROCHET

REVERS ~ COLLAR
IS STRAIGHT WITH
EDGES TURNED BACK

Fig 59

NECKLINES

'V' ~ SHAPE

BOAT SHAPE

ROUND

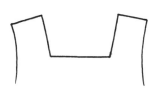

SQUARE

Fig 60

SLEEVES

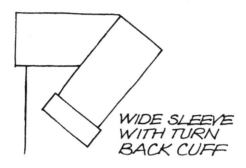

BELL SHAPE ~
WIDE SLEEVE
INTO SMALL CUFF

WIDE SLEEVE
WITH TURN
BACK CUFF

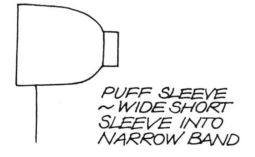

PUFF SLEEVE
~ WIDE SHORT
SLEEVE INTO
NARROW BAND

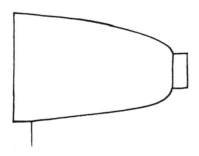

DOLMAN SLEEVE
WITH DEEP
ARMHOLE

Fig 61

Design 1: Easy Waistcoat in Three Colours (page 90); Design 8: Shawl in Picot Stitch (page 100)

POCKETS

PATCH

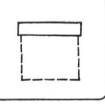

WELT~EDGING IS CROCHETED TO FRONT SIDE. POCKET PIECE IS UNDERNEATH

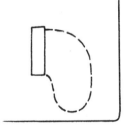

SLIT POCKET~ USEFUL WHEN GARMENT IS MADE SIDEWAYS. SHAPED BACK POCKET IS UNDERNEATH

Design 11: Textured Jumper in Three Colours (page 105); the lower inset square shows slash stitch in cream and brown which might be used as an alternative for this garment, worked as follows:

Rows 1 to 5 Using colour A (cream) work 5 rows in dc.
Row 6 Using colour B (brown) 1dc, *insert hook into st 4 rows down and complete 1dc, repeat 3 rows down, repeat 2 rows down, repeat 1 row down, 1dc. Repeat from * to end of row.
Rows 7 to 9 Work in dc.
Row 10 Using colour A, 3dc and work as for row 6 making the long st in colour A over the short st of colour B giving a diamond effect. 2 colours are used for this sample, but it could be worked in stripes of 3 or more colours.

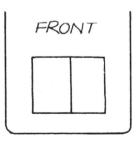

FRONT

DOUBLE POCKET ~ OPENINGS AT SIDE

Fig 62

Designing with Colour

The easiest and probably the most dramatic way of introducing colour into your designs is to use it in large blocks.

These ideas of bold use of colour are just to start you off but you will be able to think of many more – the variations are endless. Make odd shapes of different colours and crochet them to a background. Children might like to make a picture with several working on the same project.

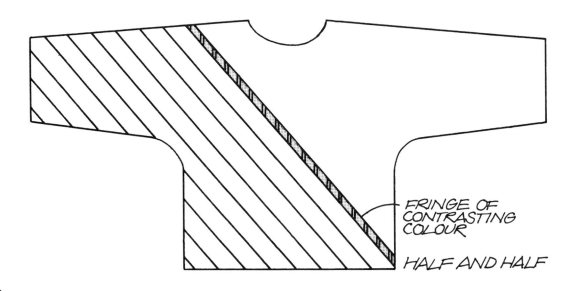

Fig 63

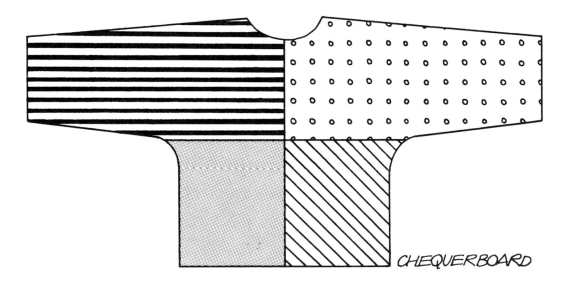

Fig 64

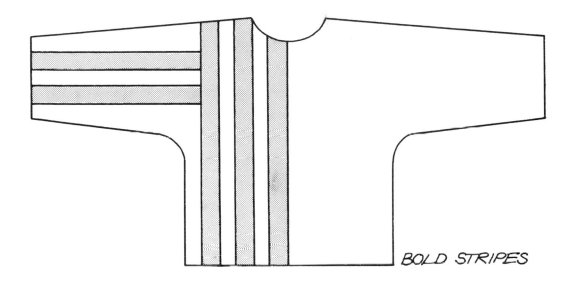

BOLD STRIPES

Fig 65

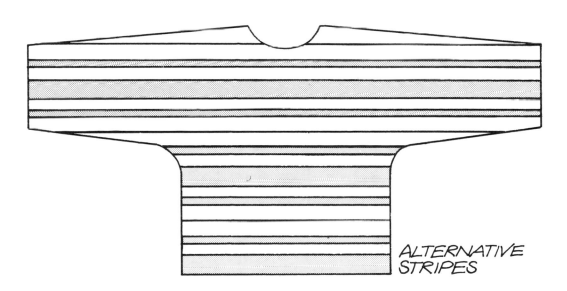

ALTERNATIVE
STRIPES

Fig 66

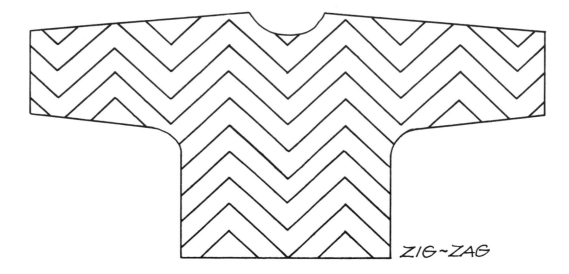

ZIG~ZAG

Fig 67

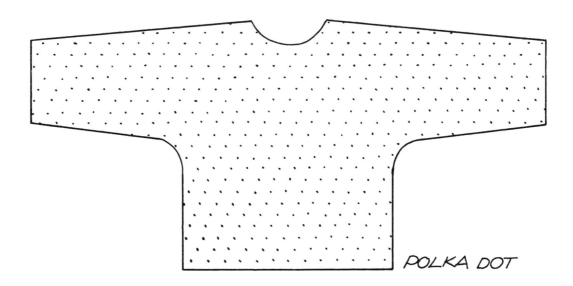

POLKA DOT

Fig 68

Ideas for Detailed Use of Colour

1   Work two rows of each colour in whatever stitch you are using. Carry the threads along the side of the work.
2   Use three colours and work one row of each colour.
3   Use three colours and work double crochet inserting the hook into the back loop of the stitch. Work one row of each colour (see Design 14, page 110).
4   Use four colours. Work one row of each colour picking up the thread which is ready to use at the end of the row. When several rows have been worked an interesting stripe pattern emerges.
5   Use 1dc 1ch as the stitch, working the double crochet into the single chain space. Use three colours so that it is possible to work one row of each colour without joining on. This gives a small check effect.
6   Weave patterns through your crochet with a coloured yarn.

Experiment with any stitches you know and any colours you have. Crochet all your samples together and make a bag to give you a ready to hand sampler of your ideas.

Texture

Texture in crochet can be achieved with a textured yarn or a textured stitch. There are many beautiful yarns available which are attractive combinations of both yarn and colour but unfortunately they are expensive. A textured yarn needs a simple repetitive stitch as the effect comes from the yarn. A complicated stitch just detracts from the beauty of the yarn and neither the stitch nor the yarn are seen to their full advantage.

Many wool firms are unfamiliar with crochet and so they recommend hooks which are too small. Bouclé yarn worked on a hook which is too small gives a fabric rather like towelling. Experiment with hook and yarn and if the fabric you make is hard and perhaps stiff, try a larger hook. Before starting any garment in textured yarn, try several hook sizes and, having made a fabric you like, sort out the tension before starting the garment.

Textured Stitches

There are literally hundreds of stitch patterns in crochet and more are being invented and discovered all the time. As a general rule the lacy stitches are most suitable in cotton and thinner yarns for more delicate garments or lace, but they are also useful in thicker yarns for shawls. The lacy stitches are not as fashionable now for jackets and waistcoats as they were twenty years ago. Now the stitch is simpler and the accent is on texture rather than pattern. At this stage it is a good idea to start a book of samples. In Victorian times crocheters kept books of their sample stitches and exchanged patterns with their friends just as we exchange recipes today. These patterns were not written down but copied and mounted in a book. These sample books are now being sought after by collectors. Mount your stitch samples in one of the attractive modern photograph albums and start your own family heirloom.

Try any of the following stitch patterns:

Popcorn Stitch

Make 14ch.

Row 1 1tr into 4th ch and tr to end of row, 3ch, turn.

Row 2 2tr, 1 popcorn (made as follows – 5tr into next st, withdraw hook and insert into 1st of 5tr; pick up dropped lp and work 2lps together with a sl st), 4tr, 1 popcorn, 3tr, 3ch, turn.

Row 3 Tr into every st, 3ch, turn.

Row 4 5tr, 1 popcorn st, 5tr, 3ch, turn.

Row 4 As Row 3.

Judith Stitch
Make a number of ch divisible by 4 plus 2ch, 1ch, turn.
Row 1 Work one row of dc, 3ch, turn.
Row 2 *Miss next st, 1tr into each of next 3st, yrh, insert hook from front to back into the missed st and work a tr. Repeat from * to end, 1tr, 1ch, turn.
Rows 1 and 2 form pattern

Openwork Squares
Make a ch a multiple of 4 plus 3.
Row 1 3ch, *2tr (1tr3ch 1dc) in next st, miss 1st. Repeat from * to end of row finishing with 3tr, 3ch, turn.
Row 2 (3tr 3ch 1dc) in 3ch sp of each motif. Finish row with 1tr in last ch, 3ch, turn.
Row 2 forms pattern

Cable Stitch
This design has the raised trebles crossed as the stitches are in a knitted cable. It is very effective if the cable is worked in a contrasting colour.
Make 18ch.
Row 1 1tr into 4th ch and tr to end of ch, 1ch, turn.
Row 2 1dc into 2nd st (place hook under the bar of the tr and work 1RtrF) 4 times, 4dc, 4RtrF, 2dc, 1ch, turn.

Row 3 1dc into 2nd st, *(place hook in front of the bar of the next and work 1RtrB) 4 times, 4dc. Repeat from * but finish with 2dc, 1ch, turn.
Row 4 1dc into 2nd st, miss 2st crossing over 2 missed tr, 2RtrF, return to 2 missed st and work 2RtrF (1 cable) 4dc, 1 cable, 2dc, 1ch, turn.
Row 5 As Row 3.
Row 6 As Row 2.
Row 7 As Row 3.
Rows 2 to 7 form pattern

Further Suggestions
Now try any of the following to make a textured effect.
1   Stitches of different length, eg 1dc, 1dtr, alternating. This makes a good border or a hat brim.
2   Basket stitch from raised trebles.
3   Spike or slash stitch of different colours on a double chain base. Drop the stitch down one, two, three or four rows.
4   Achieve looped effect by crocheting over a ruler.

Introduce different colours and textured yarn into these samples (see colour illustration, page 41).

Lesson 4

BROOMSTICK CROCHET

The origins of Broomstick Crochet, or Witchcraft Lace as it is sometimes called, are obscure. The Victoria and Albert Museum and the American Museum at Bath have no record or sample of it, yet the Americans claim it as theirs because there is evidence that the early settlers used it as a quick way of making blankets. One can imagine women on the move in their covered waggons using the tools they had to hand, namely a rod or broomstick and a crochet hook to convert their spare yarn into blankets to keep their families warm. In America, Canada and Australia it is still practised as a traditional craft and is demonstrated in their rural life museums. Many attractive patterns are available in America and it is sometimes called 'Jiffy Lace' because the work grows very quickly.

In Sweden it is called Lattice Loop. It was a peasant craft which probably originated in Europe, and the technique would have been passed on from mother to daughter without any records being kept. It was a craft born of necessity and would only have been practised by poor working women. Odds and ends of handspun yarn would have been used and the finished results warm rather than beautiful. The blankets and shawls would have had constant wear and therefore would not have been treasured as heirlooms. Thus, as with all textile crafts, lack of evidence means that the history is conjecture rather than fact.

Equipment

The crochet hook should be a suitable size for the yarn being used. For example, use a 7.00mm or 8.00mm hook for thick chunky yarns and a 3.00mm or 4.00mm hook for finer yarns and cottons.

A very large knitting needle 25mm (1in) in diameter can be used as a 'broomstick', a piece of dowelling from a handicraft shop about 40cm (16in) long can be sanded, polished and sharpened to a point like a pencil, or the end can be sawn off an actual broomstick. A wooden draught or a toy wheel can be tacked or stuck to

the end. For finer work with thin yarn or cotton use a finer needle.

Working Method

The principle of Broomstick Crochet is to make loops of a regular size by placing them on to the broomstick and to remove them in regular groups with double crochet. The thickness of the finished fabric is decided by the number of loops grouped together. The number of double-crochet stitches in the top of the group is the same as the number of loops, eg five loops are taken off with five double crochet. A warm blanket needs four or five loops together but a floaty evening stole requires only 2 loops together. There are several ways of putting the loops on to the broomstick and taking them off, and there is no right or wrong way as long as the finished work is pleasing and with a good tension. Each different method produces a slightly different effect. I have given the details of the method I teach first because most people find it the easiest.

To Work a Sample in the Basic Stitch

1 Use a thick yarn and large hook and make 25ch.
2 Hold broomstick under left arm. (Some people find it more comfortable to hold it between the knees.)
3 Place lp from last ch over broomstick.
4 Insert hook into 2nd ch.
5 Draw a lp through and place it over broomstick.
6 Continue making a lp into every ch (25st). Do not turn.
7 Insert hook into 1st 5lps. yrh and pull through centre of group. yrh and pull through the lp making a ch. (This chain is only worked on the 1st group.)

8 Work 5dc into 1st group of 5lps.
9 Insert hook into next 5lps, remove from broomstick and work 5dc.
10 Continue removing lps in groups of 5 to end of row.
11 Place 1p from last st on to broomstick.
12 Still working from left to right, insert hook into 2nd st and pull lp up and on to broomstick.
13 Continue pulling up lps from every st to end of row.
14 Remove lps from broomstick as before.

When you are confident the broomstick can be removed at the end of the first row. The loops will remain in place but care must be taken not to twist them the wrong way.

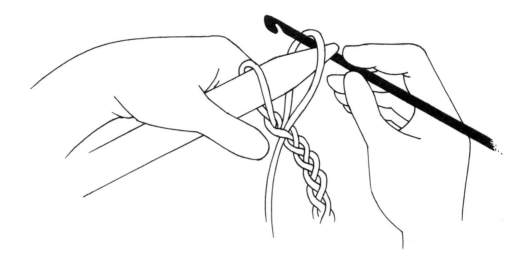

Fig 69

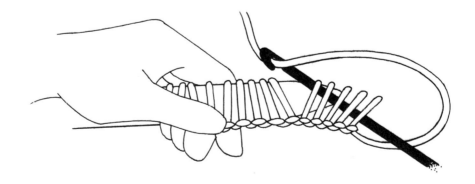

Fig 70

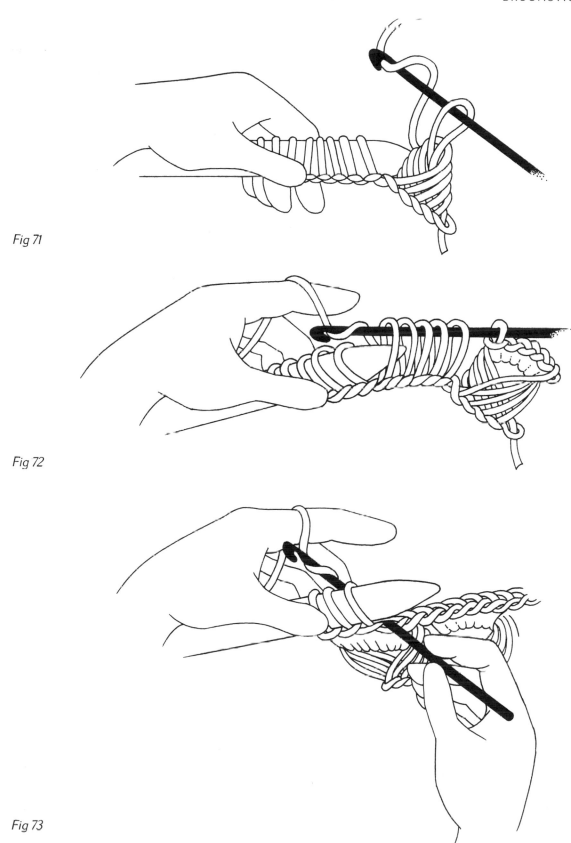

Fig 71

Fig 72

Fig 73

Stitch Variations

1   Insert the hook into the back loop of the double chain. This gives a nice rope-stitch effect.
2   Twist the loops from left to right by putting the crochet hook through the loops from left to right.
3   Twist one group of loops from right to left and the next group from left to right. Over a large area this gives an arrowhead effect.

Although there are few variations the finished results can look entirely different depending on the type of yarn used and the number of loops removed together. A blanket or a jacket needs a thick fabric with four or five loops taken off together in a thick yarn. A stole or bedjacket in a mohair-type yarn looks pretty with only two loops together. On the other hand two loops together in a fine 3 ply yarn is not very attractive. It is a question of experimenting to get the effect you like.

Shaping

Broomstick crochet is best used for garments made from very simple shapes. It is impossible to attempt to 'set in' a sleeve, for instance, but a sleeve with a dropped shoulder line can be quite successful.

To Shape for a Shawl

1   Start at the point with 5ch and 5lps.
2   Into the lps work 10dc and then 10lps.
3   Remove the 10lps in two groups of five with 10dc in each group. (This will give 20lps.)
4   Remove lps with 10dc into 1st group, 2 groups with 5dc and 10dc into the last 5lps.
5   Continue increasing with 10dc into 5lps at each end of row until the shawl is as large as you would like it.

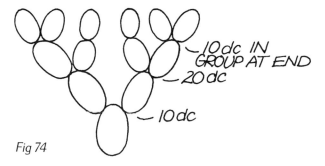

Fig 74

To Shape in a Curve

(For a round yoke or a collar)
1   Make a chain the required length for the neck and pull up lps to a number divisible by three.
2   Remove lps in groups of three with 4dc in each group.
3   Remove lps of next row in groups of four with 5dc in each group.
4   Remove lps in groups of five with 6dc.

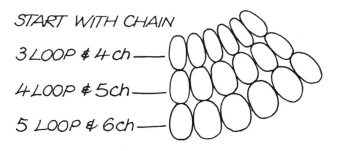

Fig 75

Worked in a thick cotton and using a 20mm (¾in) broomstick this makes a very attractive collar (see opposite).

Yarn and Colour

Most yarns which are suitable for crochet are suitable for Broomstick with the exception of some mohair yarns which do not slip very easily and so are difficult to use. As there is little variation of stitch it is quite a good idea to use colour for added interest. Work rows of different colours or introduce a row of treble- or double-crochet stitch in a contrasting colour. It is just a question of experimenting with all your different ideas. Make the samples of a regular size so they can be joined together to make a scarf or blanket.

   When you have become really proficient perhaps you would like to try a blanket on a real broomstick. You will need a chair without arm rests and plenty of space to manoeuvre. Use your odd wools and make every row a different colour. Maybe your blanket could become a family heirloom!

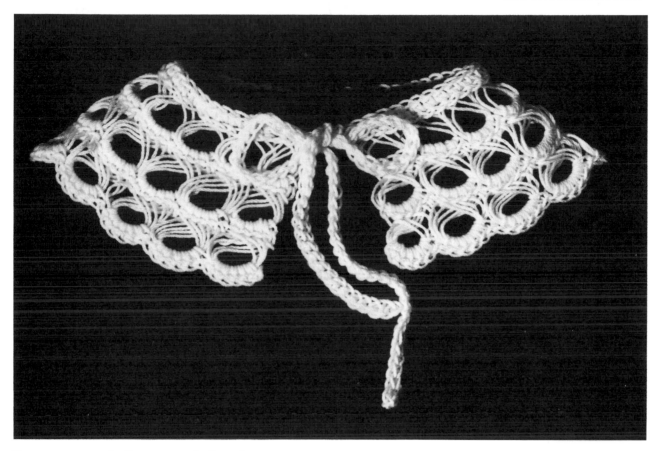

Designing with Broomstick Crochet

Broomstick Crochet needs the addition of ordinary crochet or knitting to make the edgings, welts, cuffs, etc. It can be quite a good idea to make only part of the garment in Broomstick. For instance, use Broomstick for the main part of the garment and plain crochet for the sleeves of a jacket or jumper. Alternatively, an evening jumper in a lurex and mohair yarn could have full Broomstick Crochet sleeves. The scalloped edging of Broomstick Crochet often needs no additional edge and it is possible to use one row of Broomstick as the edging for crochet or knitting. A number of designs using broomstick crochet are shown on page 66.

JACKET WITH
BROOMSTICK
YOKE, POCKETS
AND CUFFS

DETACHABLE
COLLAR

EVENING
JACKET IN
MOHAIR
WITH
BROOMSTICK
YOKE AND
SLEEVES

BROOMSTICK
SLEEVES

BATWING
JUMPER
WORKED
SIDEWAYS

TABARD FROM TWO RECTANGLES OF BROOMSTICK

Fig 76   Designs using Broomstick Crochet

Lesson 5

TUNISIAN CROCHET

Tunisian Crochet is worked with a long hook rather like a knitting needle with one end like a crochet hook. The method of working is similar to a combination of knitting and crochet, working crochet stitches but retaining the last loop of each stitch on the hook and casting off the loops on the next row. This makes a firm thick fabric suitable for warm garments and blankets.

It is a very old craft practised before knitting and crochet and perhaps even before weaving. It has also been called Russian Work and Afghan Stitch and this seems to suggest that it was practised in the countries bordering on the Mediterranean. An early example of a sock with a separate toe was found in one of the Egyptian tombs. There is also evidence that it was practised in Peru. Could the early explorers travelling from the Middle East to South America have taken it with them?

It is said that the Berber shepherds of North Africa still practise it and this is why it is sometimes known as Shepherd's Knitting. A Tunisian hook was probably a very useful tool for early nomadic man, a stick or long bone being easily shaped like a hook at one end. If a round object was placed on the other end it would make a useful drop spindle for spinning and a Berber shepherd would have plenty of available fleece to spin. One can imagine that this would have been the perfect tool to convert the wool from the sheep's back to a warm blanket to keep the cold out at night and the sun off by day.

The fabric produced with the Tunisian hook is a very thick cloth of double thickness; consequently it does take much more wool than either knitting or crochet but it is extremely firm and warm. Although originally used for blankets and rugs, the Victorians used it for bath mats, men's waistcoats and jackets. They invented a very long needle made in three parts which would screw together to make a hook about 75cm (30in) long called a blanket needle. This must have been tiring and very tedious to use.

The stitch patterns make a very attractive, close-textured fabric but some of them make a fabric which is slightly warped and is not really suitable for garments.

One can imagine that when they were originally used for blankets warmth was more important than shape.

The Americans are very keen on Tunisian Crochet which they call Afghan Work. All knee rugs in America are now called Afghans and these were originally made in panels which were then embroidered in cross stitch using the squares formed by the stitch as a cross-stitch canvas. The panels were then sewn or crocheted together. In Britain today little is known of Tunisian Crochet, most wool shops do not sell the hooks because they do not know how to use them and patterns are virtually unobtainable. Thus Tunisian Crochet is waiting to be discovered as an exciting new craft. Perhaps this lesson will encourage some of you to make a start and explore its possibilities. With all the colourful new yarns available it is possible to make exciting jackets and tops very quickly.

Working Method

Any yarn or wool used for crochet would be suitable. The work is crocheted from right to left which makes the stitch-pattern row. The return row is worked from left to right. This row casts off all the stitches on the hook leaving just one stitch to start the next row. Always work with the right side facing you. When using mohair or textured yarns the texture or fluffiness tends to be at the back on the wrong side. Sometimes the wrong side of the fabric is more attractive than the right side. If this is so make the garment up inside out!

Choosing a Hook
Hooks are made in sizes from 2.50mm to 10.00mm. Use a hook two or three sizes larger than you would for ordinary crochet; if the work is thick and tight choose a larger hook. Work the edgings in ordinary crochet with a smaller hook.

Shaping – Increasing and Decreasing
Work as for ordinary crochet but remember to keep the last loop of the stitch on the hook. It is not possible to

work 'in the round' as in ordinary crochet and it is more satisfactory to choose patterns designed with few seams. Joining the seams together with double crochet (or slip stitch) is satisfactory and gives a decorative result.

Tunisian Stitches

Before starting a garment practise by making a large square of at least 30cm (12in) to make sure the stitch does not warp. The warping is not very apparent in a small sample. In a garment such as a jumper with few openings the crochet edgings will be sufficient to hold the shape but front openings on jackets will always twist if you have chosen one of the 'warping' stitches.

Tunisian Double Crochet/Tunisian Simple (Tdc)

Make a chain the desired length.

Row 1 Insert hook into 2nd ch, yrh and pull through. Retain this lp on hook. *Insert hook into 3rd ch, yrh and pull through retaining lp on hook. Repeat from * into every ch. (Note that the hook is inserted into the top of the chain stitch and not the bottom as in ordinary crochet.)

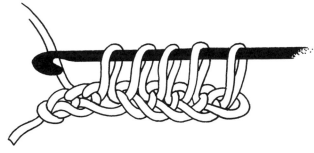

Fig 77

Row 2 *(return row)* yrh and pull through 1lp. *yrh and pull through 2lps. Repeat from * to end of row until 1lp is left on hook. The lp left on hook is the first st of next row. (This row and every alternate row is worked in this way with the exception of a few lacy stitches.)

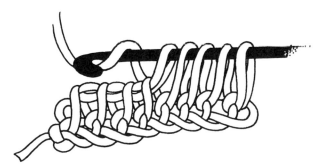

Fig 78

Row 3 Insert hook into 2nd vertical lp, yrh and pull through retaining the lp on hook. Repeat to end of row. *Rows 2 and 3 form pattern*

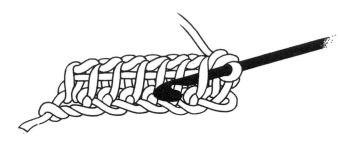

Fig 79

Tunisian Treble (Ttr)

This stitch has three standing chain which count as the first stitch.

Row 1 yrh, insert hook into 2nd vertical lp, yrh and pull through (3lps), yrh and pull through 2lps, yrh and pull through 1lp, leaving last lp on hook.

Row 2 *(return row)* Work in the usual manner as already explained.

Tunisian Double Treble (Tdtr)

Works as for Tunisian treble but with 1 extra yrh and 1 extra tch.

Tunisian Triple Treble (Ttr tr)

Work as for Tunisian treble but with 2 extra yrh and 2 extra tch.

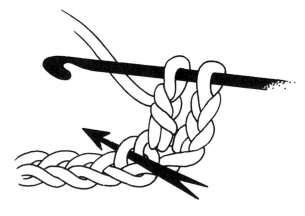

Fig 80

Tunisian Bobble Stitch (Tb)

Make a multiple of 6ch plus 4ch.
Work 1st 2 rows of Tdc.
Row 3 1Tdc, *1 bobble (made as follows – yrh, insert hook from front to back into next st [yrh pull through 1lp] 3 times, yrh and pull through 6lps, yrh and pull through 1lp), 5Tdc. Repeat from * working 1 bobble into 2nd to last st.
Rows 4 to 8 Tdc.
Row 9 4Tdc, *1 bobble into next st, 5Tdc. Repeat from * to end of row ending with 1Tdc.
Row 10 Return row.

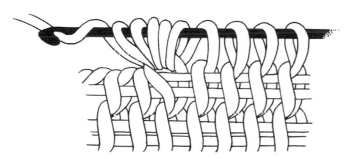

Fig 81

Plain Tunisian Stitch

Make a length of ch and work first 2 rows as Tdc.
Row 3 Miss 1st 2 vertical threads, *insert hook from front to back of work between next 2 vertical threads and under ch of previous row, yrh pull 1lp through. Repeat from * to end of row working last st between next to last st of previous row and end st.
Row 4 Return row.

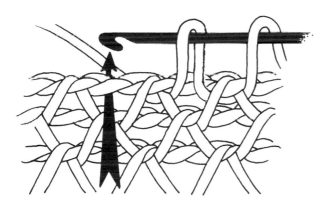

Fig 82

Row 5 Miss 1 vertical threads (2st), *insert hook from front to back of work between next 2 vertical threads under ch of previous row, yrh, pull through 1lp. Repeat from * to end working 1st into edge lp of return row.
Row 6 Tunisian return row.
Rows 3 to 6 form pattern

The fabric made with this stitch tends to curl up but firm double crochet edges will hold it to shape.

Tunisian Dropped Treble (Tdp tr) *2 colours*

Work 2 rows of Tunisian treble and the corresponding return rows (4 rows in all) in colour A.
Row 5 Using colour B miss 1st vertical thread, *1Ttr into 2nd vertical lp of the last row but one, 1Tdc into next st. Repeat from * to end of row.
Row 6 Return row.
Row 7 Using colour A work 1Tdc over Ttr of previous outward row and 1Ttr over Tdc of last row but one. Repeat to end of row.
Row 8 Return row.
Rows 5 to 8 form pattern

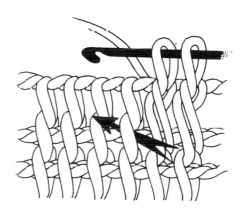

Fig 83

Tunisian Stocking Stitch (Tss)

This stitch is worked in the same way as Tunisian double crochet except for the position of the hook.

Row 1 Insert hook into centre of vertical lp, under ch row, going from front to back.

Row 2 *(return row)* Work in the usual way.

This makes a firm non-elastic fabric which is much thicker than ordinary knitting. Use a hook two sizes larger than you would for ordinary crochet to avoid a hard fabric.

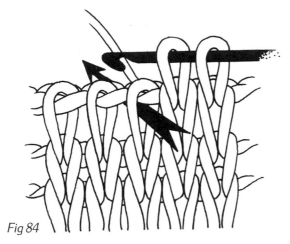

Fig 84

Tunisian Purl Stitch (Tp)

Work Row 1 and return row as for Tunisian double crochet.

Row 3 Miss 1st vertical thread, *bring yarn to front, insert hook from right to left under 2nd vertical lp. Pass yarn across front of stitch and up behind hook, yrh and pull through. Repeat from * into every stitch.

This makes a firm thick fabric which looks like a knitted purl stitch on both sides.

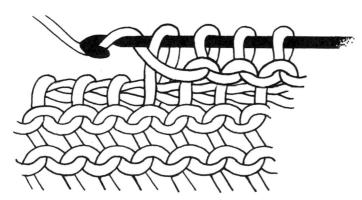

Fig 85

Design 3: Tabard or Over-jumper (page 92); Design 10: Man's Sweater (page 103)

Tunisian Rib Stitch
Make a length of ch and work 2 rows Tdc.
Row 3 Miss 1st 5 vertical threads (2½st), *yrh, insert hook from front to back into next st, yrh, pull through, miss next 4 vertical threads, yrh, insert hook into next st and pull through. Repeat from * to end of row.
Row 4 Tunisian return row.
Rows 3 and 4 form pattern

It is advisable to check number of stitches every other row until the working becomes automatic.

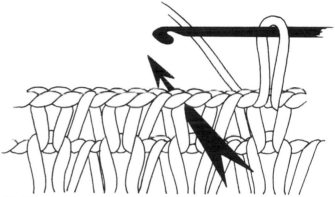

Fig 86

Slash Stitch
Make a multiple of 4ch plus 3ch.
Rows 1 to 8 Tdc.
Row 9 Change colour, *insert hook from front to back under the ch of previous dc row, yrh, pull through, yrh, pull through 1lp, repeat from * working 1st 4 rows down, 1st 6 rows down, 1st under the top ch.
Row 10 Tdc.
Rows 3 to 10 form pattern repeat

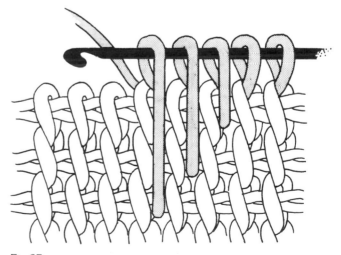

Design 4: Jacket for Beginners (page 95)

Fig 87

Casting off

In Tunisian crochet it is necessary to 'cast off' to give a firm edge for sewing up or to prevent the work curling up. This can be done simply by working one row of slip stitch or double crochet in the usual way on the vertical loop.

Tunisian Crochet as a Fabric

Tunisian Crochet can be used as a fabric for coats and jackets. Use a dressmaking pattern which has no darts. The fabric is so firm it will not run or ladder. Machine together with the stitch used for stretch fabrics with a very narrow seam allowance. Neaten the seams with zigzag or overlocking stitches. A woven braid as sold in haberdashery shops makes an attractive binding for the edges.

Colour in Tunisian Crochet

Two rows of a second colour will give a stripe if the colour is changed at the right side edge, or if the new colour is introduced at the left side an unusual woven effect is obtained. Experiment with stitches and colours.

Work two rows of a number of colours changing the new colour at the beginning of the return row on the left.

Try any of the following:

1   One row of Tunisian treble and one row of Tunisian double crochet using two colours and changing the colour on the left.

2   One row of Tunisian treble and two rows of Tunisian double crochet. Use four colours. This will give a very attractive weave with the wide Tunisian treble stripe a different colour every time.

3   Mix the stitches and work every row a different stitch.

4   Mix the stitches and colours changing the colours on the left and working two rows of every colour.

5   Use different stitches together to make a textured fabric—for example, 2 purl, 2 stocking stitch or 2 dropped trebles and 2 purl (see page 41 and 44 sample patterns).

These are modern interpretations of the old craft and there is no limit to the experimenting you can do. Some stitches you will like more than others but whatever you make it will be exclusive.

Lesson 6
FINISHING OFF

This stage is really the most important for a well-finished garment. Many well-made items are ruined by sloppy sewing up and edgings. When the individual pieces of the garment are made many people think that it is finished, apart from sewing up, which will take half an hour or so. How wrong can you be! There is a world of difference between a home-made garment which looks the work of an amateur and one which looks expensive and professionally made simply because it has been carefully sewn together. It is well worth spending time at this stage to achieve the latter.

Running in Ends

All knots must be undone and the ends threaded through a wool needle and run in invisibly. Sometimes it is possible to leave a long end which can be used for sewing up. Neatening the ends is a very boring business and if you are using a lot of colours it is a good idea to tackle them as you go along rather than leave the mammoth task until the end.

Pressing

Always read the instructions given on the wool bands. The manufacturers will have thoroughly tested the yarn and know how it should be treated. If in any doubt do not press crochet and if you do press *never* use a damp cloth. The attraction of crochet is the interesting texture of the fabric and any hard pressing completely destroys this. Acrilan and many other man-made yarns will be ruined because the heat actually melts them and moisture stretches them. If you feel you want to press use only a warm iron with a dry cloth. Some designs with white cotton using a very lacy pattern are actually starched and pressed out with a damp cloth but the design instructions will give details of how to do this. Again it must be stressed that, if in any doubt about pressing, do not do so. A well made garment will be perfectly all right with a very light pressing just on the seams and edgings.

Blocking

An ironing board is usually not large enough. You need an old table where the work can lie undisturbed for a day or two. Protect the table with newspapers and pad with an old blanket, finally covering with an old clean sheet. Place the garment pieces right sides down and pull into shape and pin to the blanket base. Check the measurements and make sure your garment pieces match up. If you are not pressing cover with a damp cloth and leave until the cloth is dry.

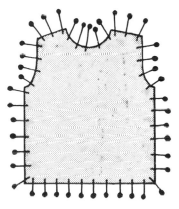

Fig 88

Sewing Up

There are several ways of putting your garment together and it might be worthwhile experimenting with your tension square to see which is the best method for the yarn you are using.
Double crochet This is often a good method to use with fancy yarns particularly multi-coloured yarns. Double-crochet joins can also be used on the right side possibly in a contrasting colour as a decoration.
Slip stitch should be worked on the wrong side. This makes a flat seam which has a certain amount of elasticity.

Over-sewing This is most frequently used but care must be taken so that the stitches blend in and do not show on the right side. When sewing up stripes have as many sewing needles as you have colours so you can sew with the colour of the stripe and slip along on the wrong side over the stripes of a different colour. The stitches will then not show on the stripes.

Back stitching This makes a very strong seam. It is very bulky but useful for sewing uneven edges together.

Weaving This is worked on the right side and is only possible if the edges are straight or interlocking. It is very good for matching patterns and giving a flat finish. Place the edges, right sides facing, together and weave from side to side making the stitch design match.

Sewing by Machine

This will make a bulky seam and if sewing a fitted sleeve for instance it is possible to obtain a very smart finish. The big disadvantage is that it is terribly difficult to unpick. It is very necessary to be absolutely sure of your seam position before machining. It is very useful for 'cut and sew' methods of altering garments, using the crochet as a fabric.

Setting in Shaped Sleeves

First sew the shoulder seams of garment, then the side seams and the sleeve seams. Turn the garment inside out and drop the sleeve into the armhole matching the centre point of the sleeve head to the shoulder seam and the side seam to the underarm seam of the sleeve. If the sleeve head is rather full ease it into the armhole. A row of gathering will pull it up if necessary. Mould the head of the sleeve over a pad to give a smart finish.

Edgings

Explicit instructions on how to do edgings are seldom given in commercial patterns, and yet they are most important to the finished look of the garment. A bungled edge can completely ruin a garment so it is most important to take extreme care and plenty of time. One of the most difficult tasks is to pick up the same number of stitches on each side of the front and neck edges. Do not go on with the second row until you have done this. Always use a hook a size smaller than that used for the main garment.

Increasing and Decreasing

Commercial patterns usually ignore the shaping needed to keep the edging flat. All the increasing and decreasing needed for the neck, fronts and bottom edges would need such a lot of detailed explanation. With experience and by experimenting you will soon know how to do this. A right-angled corner will need three double chain into one stitch in each row to get round the corner. A more gradual corner as on the front neck of a cardigan will need two stitches in one. It will be necessary to decrease two into one about three times to make a neck edge lie flat. It is difficult to be specific about the decreasings but by a little trial and error success will be achieved.

A Double-crochet Edge

Most commercial patterns just say work four or six rows of double crochet with no further instructions. Consequently the crocheter works the rows not turning the work, if the edge goes right round all the edges of the garment. This makes a nice smooth stitch but the edge will curl at the bottom corners. To prevent this always complete each round with a slip stitch, one turning chain, turn the work and work in the opposite direction.

A Simple Treble Edge

Row 1 Work 1 row of tr decreasing and increasing in the necessary places.

Row 2 1tr, 1ch, miss 1st, repeat to end of row.

Row 3 1 row of tr decreasing over the increases of the 1st row and increasing over the decreases. Fold back so that 2nd row makes a picot edging and sew into place (see Design 4, page 95).

A Decorative Edge of Pineapple Stitch

Row 1 Work 1 row of dc. Change to yarn of contrasting colour or texture.

Row 2 3ch, *1 htr (yrh and place hook sideways under the htr bar, yrh and pull through), repeat 3 more times, yrh and pull through all the lps, miss 1st. Repeat from * to end of row. Sl st to top of 3ch. Change to original yarn.

Row 3 2dc into every sp between the bobbles.

There are an infinite number of edges which you can discover for yourself. Introduce ribbon or leather and thread it through spaces, but remember a very patterned or colourful garment needs a fairly plain edging whereas a plain stitch will take a complicated or colourful edging.

Crab Stitch

This stitch is sometimes called Shrimp Stitch, Russian Stitch or simply Reverse Double Crochet. It makes a very pleasing edge to the double-crochet edging. Commercial patterns do not give details of how to do the stitch and books of stitch instructions just dismiss it as double crochet worked from left to right instead of right to left. This is true but it does not quite explain how it is worked.

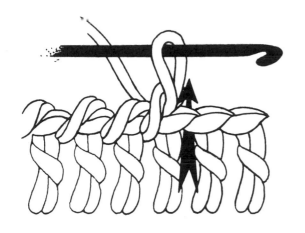

Fig 89

Hairpin Crochet

There seems to be no evidence to suggest that this is any earlier than Victorian. It was used chiefly as an edging but it can be crocheted or looped together to form a lacy fabric. The method of doing this is too lengthy to describe here but it is useful to learn how to make a braid very quickly which can be used for decoration on dresses, edgings or upholstery.

Hairpins or Prongs

These are anything from 2cm (¾in) to 7.5cm (3in). Hairpin looms or quad frames are sometimes available for much larger projects. In Victorian times very dainty lace could be made on actual hairpins with very fine cotton.

Method
(to make a 2.5cm [1in] braid)
Use 2.5cm (1in) hairpin and wool or cotton of 4 ply or double-crochet thickness. Hold the hairpin in the left hand. It is quite correct to have the prongs either at the top or the bottom. When using the prongs upwards it is possible to keep the loop in the hook when turning the hairpin and I find this gives a better tension.
1   Make a lp and place over prongs of hairpin.

Method

1   Make 1 standing ch, hold hook at right angles to the body and insert hook through st from front to back, yrh and pull through changing the position of the hook.
2   Lift it up turning it sideways facing to the left parallel with the edge, yrh and pull through.

It is changing position of the hook which gives this stitch. The attractive corded edging can be worked in a contrasting colour.

Crab Stitch as a decorative corded edging Work one row of Crab Stitch in a contrasting colour on the front loop of the stitch. Break off the original colour and rejoin to the right-hand side and work one row of double crochet from right to left in the usual manner picking up the back loop of the last double crochet row. It is not necessary to rejoin the yarn if the edgings are being worked 'in the round'. The edging can be left like this as it is quite an attractive finish. Rows of double crochet can be continued until the second half is as wide as the first. It can then be sewn back into position leaving the Crab Stitch on the extreme edge. This edge does not curl up.

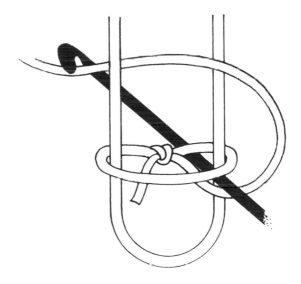

Fig 90

2   Secure this lp with 1 ch st. (All the stitches are worked on the left loop only and after every group of stitches turn the hairpin from right to left. This forms a loop on the right prong.)

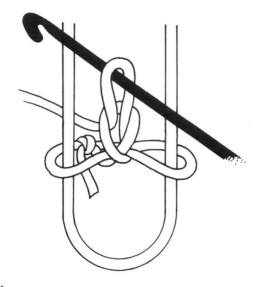

Fig 91

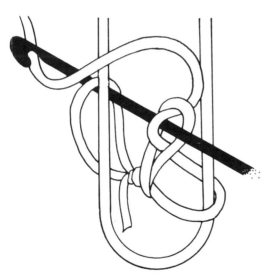

Fig 92

3   Turn prong from right to left and secure new lp with 1dc.
4   Work 3dc into centre of lp on left prong.
5   Turn prong from right to left – secure new lp with 1dc in the centre.
6   Work 3dc on left loop.
7   Continue working in this way until braid is the length you require.

It is possible to experiment with different numbers of stitches and mix with ordinary crochet.

Fastenings

Crochet does not lend itself very well to modern fastenings. Hooks and velcro will catch on the loops. Zips for the fronts of jackets or sides of skirts are quite permissible but they must be very neatly sewn in, preferably by hand. It is quite a good idea to buy the open-ended zip before you even buy the yarn, and buy the yarn to match the zip. Many department stores find it uneconomical to stock open-ended zips. It is very frustrating to finish a garment and then find a zip the correct size or colour is unobtainable in your area.

Buttonholes

These are very easy to work in crochet. The most difficult part is to sort out the spacing down the front edge. With paper and pencil and the total number of stitches down the edge you must work out how many buttonholes you need, how big they have to be for the buttons you have chosen and how many stitches you need at the top and bottom of the edge. Commercial patterns seldom do this for you. For example, make 3 chain and miss 3 stitches. Work the 3 chain as stitches on the return row. For a smaller button use 2 chain. Buttonholes should be fairly tight as they tend to wear loose. It is a good idea to buttonhole stitch around so that they keep their size and do not stretch with wear.

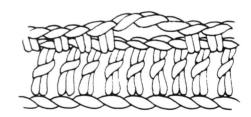

Fig 93

Buttonhole Loops

Can be worked on the edge by working loops of chain stitch and working buttonhole stitch several times into the loop.

Welt Pockets

These are worked in the same way as buttonholes but by making more chain and leaving more stitches. Complete the pocket by making an edging on the front side of the pocket and crocheting a pocket piece for the back of the pocket (see Tunisian jacket Design 21, page 123).

Buttons

It is very difficult to choose buttons which look right on crochet garments. Large beads often make a good alternative. Antique pearl or bone ones are very good. Remember with crochet it has to look like or be the real thing. Modern plastic will not do, but it is quite easy to make your own.

Crochet Buttons

These are very easy to make and will save you money. Once you have made them successfully you will be able to experiment with lots of ideas and so give your garments an exclusive look.

Method

Wind the yarn twice round your index finger, insert the hook and work 5 or 6dc. Pull the end tight so that there is no hole in the centre. Increase twice into each stitch. Use an old plastic button as a mould and place this in position on your circle of crochet which must be visible all round. Decrease on the next round. Break the yarn and thread a sewing needle. Gather up the centre and make a loop for sewing on the button.

Here are some variations:
1   Try making the hole in the centre of the button larger, using colourful beads or pearls which show.
2   Embroider the buttons with beads or coloured yarn.
3   Use different colours, remembering the rule of contrast, ie colourful decorated buttons on a garment of one colour and plain buttons on multi-coloured garments.

Dorset Buttons

Brass or plastic rings are needed for the outside base of the button.

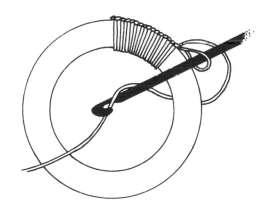

Fig 94

1   Thread a needle with a long piece of yarn, place the end along the ring and work over it with buttonhole stitch to secure it.
2   When the ring is complete push the knots round the ring to the centre.
3   Wind 'spokes' across the ring and secure them in the centre.
4   Working from right to left backstitch over the 'spokes' of the wheel taking 1 stitch back over 1 spoke and forward under 2 spokes until the ring is filled up and looks rather like a spider's web. Work a loop on the back of the button.

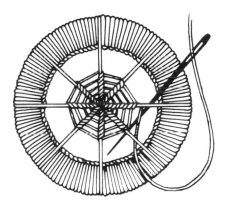

Fig 95

String, Cords and Ropes

These can be used as tie belts for garments, strings to pull up necks, waists, etc and handles for bags.

Twisted Cord

This is the easiest way of making a cord and children love making them because they twist up like magic.
1   Cut strands of yarn about three times as long as you need the finished cord. Four strands make a thin cord. A rope will need eight or more.
2   One person holds each end and twists clockwise, until it is twisted up very tightly.
3   Place the ends together, hold the centre and the cord will spring up into a twist.
4   Tie a knot in each end and cut into two even tassels.

Double-crochet Cord

1   Wind yarn round index finger twice and work 5dc into the lp.
2   Continue working 1dc into every st until cord is as long as required.
3   Thread a wool needle and finish off.
4   Thread starting end through wool needle, pull and finish off.

Slip Stitch on Chain
1 Make a chain the length of the cord needed.
2 Slip stitch into each chain.

For a two-colour cord use double yarn together and work a chain in alternate colours.

Woven Cord in Two Colours
1 Tie the two colours together and make a slip knot in colour A.

Fig 96

2 Put index finger of right hand through slip knot.
3 With finger facing to the left 'dig' down and pull through colour B.
4 Place index fingers end to end and transfer new loop to left index finger.
5 Pull end of colour A tight with right hand.
6 Dig down with left finger and pull up colour A and transfer loop to right finger.
7 Pull tight colour B with the left hand.

Continue working, transferring the loops from the right index finger to the left and pulling the ends tight with alternate hands. As you practise this the tension will improve but if you stop in the middle of the cord it will show. This makes a very attractive cord with a number of uses.

By experimenting with lengths of double-crocheted chain you will discover an enormous number of variations.

(opposite)
Design 14: Blouson Jacket in Three Colours (page 110); the lower inset square shows an alternative dropped treble pattern in grey and pink which might be used as an alternative for this garment, worked as follows:
Using colour A (grey) make an odd number of ch.
Row 1 Tr.
Row 2 Dc.
Row 3 Using colour B (pink) 3tch, *1dtr worked around the bar of the tr st 2 rows down. 1tr. Repeat from * to end of row.
Row 4 Dc.
Row 5 Colour A, as row 3.
Row 6 Dc.
Rows 3 to 6 form the pattern.

(overleaf left)
Design 19: Jacket and Waistcoat in Tunisian Crochet (page 119)

(overleaf right)
Design 18: Broomstick Crochet Waistcoat (page 118); the lower inset square shows a rust and green fan pattern which might be used as an alternative for this garment, worked as follows:
Using colour A, make a number of ch divisible by 6.
Row 1 3tch, 2tr into the 4th ch, *3ch, 5tr into the 6th st. Repeat from * to end of row, 3tr into last ch. Break off yarn. Do not turn.
Row 2 Join in colour B at beginning of row, 1dc into tch of previous row, *2ch, 1tr into base ch, 1ch, miss 1ch, 1tr into base ch, 1dc into centre tr of 5tr group. Repeat from * finishing with 1dc into last tr of previous row. Do not turn.
Row 3 Join in colour C at beginning of row, 1tch, 1dc, 1ch, 5tr into 4th st, *3ch, miss 7st, 5tr into next st. Repeat from * to end of row. Finish with 5tr into 1st ch, 1dc, turn.
Row 4 Rejoin in colour B, 3ch, 1tr into row 2, *2ch, 1dc into centre tr of group, 1tr into row 2, 1ch, miss 1st, 1tr into row 2. Repeat from * to end of row, finishing with 2tr into row 2. Do not turn.
Row 5 Rejoin in colour A and work as for row 1.
Continue working in pattern, alternating the colours and 'fans'. This stitch is far more difficult to explain than it is to work; the photograph helps to make it clearer.

Tassels, Fringes and Pompons

(For Fringes see Lesson 1)

Tassels

Cut a piece of cardboard the desired length of the tassel. Wind wool round to the thickness you want the tassel. Thread one end through a sewing needle. Sew the loops with two or three stitches at one end and then cut one end and remove card. Make the head of the tassel by winding two or three strands about 3cm (1¼in) away from top loop of tassel and finish off. Trim ends.

Pompons

Cut two cardboard circles the diameter of the finished pompon. Cut a hole in the centre of the circle. The size of the hole depends on the size of the pompon. The larger the circle the larger the central hole must be. Thread three or four long strands of yarn on to a large sewing needle. Wind the yarn around the circle until it is completely covered. Cut the outer edges taking the scissors between the two pieces of cardboard. Wind yarn round the yarn between the two cardboard discs and fasten off leaving a long end. Remove the cardboard. Fluff up the pompon and trim into shape.

How to Care for Your Garments

Lining

Owing to the lacy nature of crochet many people feel they would like their garments lined. This is often not a very good idea and if it is at all possible it is best to wear an undergarment of a complimentary colour. Fabrics are made from so many different man-made fibres and although the lining may look perfectly all right in wear it may twist or crease under the crochet. If however you decide it must be lined attach the lining at the tops of neck, waist and armhole and leave it to fall free at the bottom.

Washing

Always look at the yarn label and see if washing or dry cleaning is recommended and only wash in the washing machine if the manufacturer recommends it. If you are using several different yarns do not forget all the labels. When in doubt wash in warm water with a mild detergent or soap flakes, give a fifteen-second spin, two rinses and another fifteen-second spin just to get the bulk of the water out. Dry flat after pulling into shape. If you are in any doubt about how to treat your garment it is wiser to dry clean.

Design 12: Jackets in Bouclé Yarn (page 106)

Storing Garments

Never hang crochet garments on a hanger. The garment will 'drop' or stretch and the hanger will make holes in it. Always use a flat surface to pull the garment into shape, then fold up and store in a drawer.

Amending and Altering

Too Long

If your garment needs to be shorter because fashions have changed, if it has dropped or has just turned out too long, it is possible to cut off the bottom few rows. This sounds very drastic and most people are scared to do it but you can't go wrong providing you cut straight along the row. Pull out the remaining half stitches and work one row of double crochet or any edging suitable for the design. Sometimes with lacy patterns you get unexpectedly nice effects which need no neatening.

If you have worked a garment sideways and still want to shorten it, stitch one row of straight machining where you want the edge to be, then cut along the machined edge and work another row of machining or a zigzag row. Work one row of double crochet to cover up the machining and then an edging if you wish.

Too Short

It is always possible to add more rows but whenever you do it must look as if that is how you intended it to be in the first place. No doubt the edging will have to be unpicked first.

Too Small

Add a few rows of double crochet or treble to the underarms or wherever the garment is too small. Try and make it look as though that is part of the pattern.

Not Enough Yarn

Work edgings or yokes in a different colour or a different texture. Turn your garment into something else, ie a waistcoat instead of a jacket.

Tips for Better Crochet

Starting Off

It is very difficult to count chain. Do not count your starting chain but make a rough estimate of how long you need it and then add ten more. Work the first row and count the stitches. It is much easier to count double crochet or treble than chain. Unpick any extra chain you may have. Leave a long end from your starting loop and use that to make extra chain if you have run out. If you are working a lacy stitch first work one row of double crochet then break off the yarn leaving a longish end. Rejoin yarn to right edge and work out the stitch pattern on the double crochet. This is much easier than trying to 'set' the stitch pattern on the chain. Add extra chain or unpick any spare chain.

How to Join

It is best to make your joins at the end of the row and just tie a knot which can be undone after the garment is finished and the ends run in. If you wish to join in the middle of a row loop the two ends of yarn together and work one stitch with double yarn where they cross and run the ends in after.

Changing Colour

At the end of the row tie the new colour on to the old colour with a single knot. Work the last movement of the stitch and the turning chain in the new colour. Run in the ends before sewing up.

NOTES FOR TEACHERS

It is quite a daunting task to be faced with about twenty people, some of whom will be left handed, who have never held a crochet hook before. Details of how I cope may be of help to some teachers. At the end of one and a half or two hours, I have all the students, with hardly any exceptions, crocheting away and feeling very pleased with themselves. It is very satisfying to stand back and watch them. I think crochet is almost the only subject where you can observe the results of your efforts so quickly.

Class Arrangement

I have found this very important. Have the class seated in a semi-circle away from desks and tables and stand in the centre. The students will quickly become very friendly and helpful towards each other and it is possible to spot the person who needs extra attention at once. (Note the suggestions in Lesson 1 for left-handed students.) Make sure that every one has a 6.00mm or 7.00mm hook and thick yarn to use. Stand in the centre of the circle with your back to the class to demonstrate how to hold the yarn.

Lesson 1

Start with absolute basics of how to tie a slip knot, holding the yarn, etc. You may have to demonstrate each point three or four times. Do not go on until every one in the class has understood. It is well worth spending time at this stage. Do not allow any student to 'knit' or hold the yarn as for knitting. Each one must persevere until holding the yarn becomes quite automatic.

Always write up, so the whole class can see, the abbreviations as you come to them. By the end of two hours' instruction they should be able to tie a slip knot, hold the yarn, make an even chain, work a treble and keep the edges straight.

Suggest some of the things they can make before the next lesson such as belts, bags, scarves, etc, in fact anything which has straight edges where fit is relatively unimportant. Always finish the lesson by revising what has been learnt.

Lesson 2

Begin the lesson by discussing the work brought by the enthusiastic students who can explain how they made things and any problems they had. This is where the class members learn from each other without even realising it.

Quickly revise what they learnt the previous week, including the abbreviations. Teach simple stitch patterns. Already some students will be much better then others and they could be encouraged to read stitch patterns involving only trebles.

Lesson 3

All lessons now will automatically start with students' work and it may become difficult not to spend too much time on this. Teach the rest of the stitches by demonstration with students working their own samples. Write up all abbreviations as you go along. At this stage the students will start to read commercial patterns without realising it. They will have seen the abbreviations so many times that they understand them without looking them up.

Lesson 4

By this time some students will be really good and will no longer need formal teaching. They can do their own thing by experimenting, getting ideas from books or by individual help and instruction from the teacher. Many people will still like to sit in a semi-circle and have help from the teacher or help each other. Others will prefer to drift off to a table and work at their own pace.

Always start each lesson with a demonstration of some aspect of crochet so that in each lesson every student has learnt something. Crochet is such a varied craft and they will not all enjoy every aspect of it. You will notice the personalities of the students coming through in their preferences. For example, a slap-happy person will probably like chunky wool, a large hook and quick results whereas a neat fastidious person will prefer to make fine white lace. It does not matter — the stitches and techniques are all the same. The important thing is to be creative and achieve satisfaction with one of the most relaxing crafts there is.

The more able students are now ready to make their own designs. At this stage all the class can make the basic shape for tabards and jackets in paper to their own individual measurements. These shapes can be used as a guide for size when working from commercial patterns for those who are still not sufficiently confident to work out their own ideas. There will be a tremendous range of ability at this stage and it is most important to encourage the slower and less able person. It can be quite difficult to direct the students to work well within their capabilities and to prevent them from being too ambitious. Success is extremely important because any failures at this stage may put them off crochet for ever.

INSTRUCTIONS FOR ILLUSTRATED GARMENTS

The number in brackets after many of the designs indicates the shape used (see Lesson 3, page 31).

A lesson number is given after the title of each project; this indicates the lesson which should be mastered before the garment is tackled.

For abbreviations used in the designs see page 9.

Design 1: Easy Waistcoat in Three Colours *(Lesson 1)*
Illustrated in colour on page 53

Materials
6 × 100gm balls Twilleys Capricorn Chunky (2 balls of each of 3 colours); No 8.00mm hook

Measurements
Bust: 81cm (32in). Work 2 extra rows for each larger bust size.
Length: 64cm (25in). For longer length add 6st extra for every 3cm (1in). For length subtract 6st for every 3cm (1in).

Tension
12st and 5 rows to 10cm (4in)

Design Note
The waiscoat is made very simply from two straight strips of crochet which are folded in half and sewn together.

Left Front and Back
Make 136ch.
Row 1 (colour A) Into 4th ch from hook 1tr, 1tr into every ch. Change to colour B, 3ch, turn.
Row 2 1tr into back lp of 2nd st, 1tr into back lp of every st to end of row, 1tr into tch, change to colour C, 3ch, turn. Carry the colours along edge of work.

Row 2 forms pattern. Continue for 11 more rows, working always into back of st with 1 row of each colour.

Right Front and Back
Make 136ch and work another strip to match the first one.

Pockets (make 2)
Make 18ch in colour A.
Row 1 1tr into 4th ch from hook and tr to end of ch. Change to colour B, 3ch, turn.
Row 2 1tr into back lp of 2nd st, tr into back of every st, taking last st into tch of previous row. Change to colour C, 3ch, turn.

Work 6 more rows and finish off.

To Make Up
1 Fold strips in half and sew from bottom to within 20cm (8in) from fold. These 20cm (8in) make the armhole.
2 Place two halves together and from bottom edge sew 56cm (22in) making centre back seam.
3 With colour A work 1 row of tr along bottom edge.
4 Sew pockets in place.

Tie Belt
With colour A cut 8 strips measuring 4½m (180in). With a friend holding one end, twist up very tightly anti-clockwise and then fold in half (see Lesson 6, page 79). Tie a knot at each end and cut ends.

Design 2: Lurex Evening Top and Matching Bag (Lesson 1)
Illustrated in colour on page 112

Materials
6 × 100gm balls Twilleys Double Gold; No 6.00mm hook; 2½m (2¾yd) × 1cm (½in) velvet ribbon

Measurements
Bust: 81–87cm (32–34in). To make larger add extra rows.

Tension
16st and 8 rows to 10cm (4in)

Evening Top

Make 40ch.
Row 1 1tr into 4th ch from hook, 1tr into each ch, 3ch, turn.
Row 2 1tr into 2nd st, 1tr into every st to end of row, 1tr into tch, 3ch, turn. Repeat Row 2 26 more times.
Next Row Miss 1st, 1tr 1ch to end of row, finish with 1tr, 3ch, turn.
Next Row 1tr into every st, 3ch, turn.
Next Row As last row but one.

Repeat last two rows once more. Continue working in tr st until 28 rows have been completed. Join into a circle by working 1 row of dc into last row and the base ch at the same time.

Top Edging
3ch, turn work on its side and work 1 row of tr all round top edge. Finish off.

Bottom Edging
Row 1 Join yarn to other end of centre back seam and work 3ch and 1 row of tr all round, inserting hook into ends of rows. Sl st 1st tr, 3ch, turn.
Row 2 Work next row of 1tr, 1ch, miss 1st, sl st last st to 1st st, 3ch, turn.

Row 3 Work 1 row of tr into every st, sl st to 1st st and finish off.

Straps
Make 2 rows of ch as long as you need the straps. Into 4th ch from hook make 1tr and tr to end of chain. Finish off.

Weaving
Weave velvet ribbon through spaces down centre front of top. Turn in edges of ribbon and sew down invisibly. Weave ribbon through straps and sew straps into position.

Tie for Waist
Cut 8 strips 4½m (180in) long. With a friend holding one end, both twist anti-clockwise until it is very tight. Fold in half and let it spring into a rope. Tie a knot at each end and trim ends. Thread through the spaces at waist.

Evening Bag

Make 32ch. Work (1 row of tr and 1 row of 1tr, 1ch, miss 1st) 3 times. Continue in tr for 20 more rows and finish off. Weave 3 rows of velvet ribbon through the spaces.

To Make Up
1 Cut out a piece of stiff vilene or buckram the same size as the bag.
2 Cut a piece of lining material which is 1cm (½in) bigger than the bag all the way round.
3 Tack edges of lining material over buckram all the way round. Pin to the bag and oversew all the way round.
4 Fold bag into three inside out, leaving woven edge as the flap.
5 Oversew the two ends. Turn to right side and add snap fasteners if desired.

Design 3: Tabard or Over-jumper
(Lesson 1)
Illustrated in colour on page 71

Materials
8 × 50gm Balls Pingouin Bouclette Imprimée; 1 ball of contrast yarn of chunky thickness for belt; No 8.00mm hook; 2 large beads

Tension
10st and 5½ rows to 10cm (4in)

Measurements
Bust: 97cm (38in). Add 2st for each larger size or deduct 2st for each smaller size.
Length: 63cm (25in). Work more or less rows as required.

Back and Front (both alike)
Make 46ch.
Row 1   1tr into 4th ch from hook, 1tr into every ch, 3ch, turn.
Row 2   1tr into 2nd st, 1tr into every st, 1tr into tch, 3ch, turn.

Repeat Row 2 until work measures 63cm (25in) or length required. Finish off.

To Make Up
1   Sew shoulder seams 7.5cm (3in) from armhole.
2   Sew side seams leaving a large armhole about 23cm (9in).

Belt
Using double chunky yarn make 60ch. Thread large wool needle with a very long thread of Pingouin yarn and weave on wrong side of chain from left to right and right to left. Sew a large bead to each end.

Design 20: Tunisian Coat and Hat (page 121)

Design 4: Jacket for Beginners
(Lesson 1)
Illustrated in colour on page 72

Materials
Jacket: 8 (9, 9) × 100gm balls Twilleys Capricorn Chunky; 1 ball in contrasting colour for edging; No 6.00mm and 7.00mm hooks
Hat: 2 × 50gm balls Twilleys Capricorn Chunky; No 7.00mm and 8.00mm hooks
Measurements
Jacket: Bust: 96 (102, 107)cm; 38 (40, 42)in
Length: 64 (64, 66)cm; 25 (25, 26)in
Sleeve length: 54 (56, 59)cm; 21 (22, 23)in
Hat: To fit average-size head 56cm (22in)
Tension
10 st and 5½ rows to 10cm (4in)

Jacket

Back
With No. 7.00mm hook make 54 (57, 60)ch.
Row 1 1tr into 4th ch from hook. 1tr into each ch, 3ch, turn.
Row 2 1 tr into 2nd st, 1tr into each st to end of row, 1tr into turning ch, 3ch, turn.

Continue as Row 2 until work measures 64 (64, 66)cm; 25 (25, 26)in. Finish off.

Front (make 2)
Make 29 (30, 32)ch. Work in tr until front measures same as back.

Sleeves (make 2)
Make 46 (48, 50)ch. Work in tr until work measures 54 (56, 59)cm; 21 (22, 23)in.

Pockets (make 2)
Make 17 (18, 19)ch. Work in tr for 6 rows. Finish off.

To Make Up
1 Sew shoulder seams for 17 (18, 19)cm; 6½ (7, 7½)in.
2 Place centre of sleeve head to shoulder seam and sew in place. Repeat for other side.
3 Sew up sleeve and side seam in one operation.

(left) Design 6: Scarf with Pockets and Matching Hat (page 98); *(centre)* Design 5: Basket Stitch Hat and Scarf Set (page 97); *(right)* Design 7: Beret and Stole in Three Colours (page 99)

64 (64, 66) cm
25 (25, 26) in

54 (56, 59) cm
21 (22, 23) in

BACK

**FRONT
2**

**SLEEVES
2**

**POCKETS
2**

**15 cm
6 in**

**101 (107, 112) cm
40 (42, 44) in**

**50 (53, 56) cm
20 (21, 22) in**

**40 (42, 44) cm
16 (17, 18) in**

Edging

Row 1 With contrast yarn and No 6.00mm hook, attach yarn to centre back of neck. Work in tr all round edges of garment, joining with sl st to 1st tr, 3ch. Make 3tr into 1st st at corners.

Row 2 *1ch, miss 1st, 1tr. Repeat from * to end of round. Join with sl st, 3ch.

Row 3 1tr into every st and every sp, decreasing 3 into 1 at corners. Sew edging in halves so that the 1tr 1ch row makes picots.

Sleeves

Work edging to match on bottom of sleeves.

Pockets

Work edging to top of pocket and sew in place.

Belt

Work 1 row of tr on 150cm (60in) of ch in contrasting colour. Weave in and out every 3st with main colour. Buttonhole stitch round 2 bone rings and sew to end of belt.

Hat

With No 7.00mm hook, make 6ch, sl st into circle, 3ch.

Round 1 11tr into circle, sl st to top of standing ch, 3ch (12 bars).

Round 2 1tr into base of standing ch, 2tr into each st, sl st to top of standing ch, 3ch (24 bars).

Round 3 As Round 2 (48 bars).

Continue for 8 rounds without increasing.

Turn-back Brim

Turn hat inside out to work. Change to contrast yarn.

Round 12 With No. 8.00mm hook, yrh, place hook under bar of 1st tr bringing it out of 2nd sp. yrh, and complete the tr. yrh, from the back of work place hook into 2nd sp across the bar of 2nd tr and out of 3rd sp at the back. yrh, and complete the tr. Repeat to end of round finishing with hook under st ch, making a sl st.

Repeat Round 12 6 times. Finish off with 1 row dc.

Design 5: Basket Stitch Hat and Scarf Set (Lesson 1)

Illustrated in colour on page 94

Materials

Hat: 2 × 50gm balls Patons Husky; No 7.00mm and 8.00mm hooks

Scarf: 6 × 50gm balls Patons Husky; No 7.00mm hook

Measurements

Hat: To fit average-size head 56cm (22in)

Scarf: Make as long as desired; 18cm (7in) wide

Hat

With No 7.00mm hook, make 6ch, sl st into circle, 3ch.

Round 1 11tr into circle, sl st to top of standing ch, 3ch (12 bars).

Round 2 1tr into base of standing ch, 2tr into each st, sl st to top of standing ch, 3ch (24 bars).

Round 3 As Round 2 (48 bars).

Continue for 8 rounds without increasing.

Turn-back Brim

Turn hat inside out to work.

Round 12 With No. 8.00mm hook, yrh, place hook under bar of 1st tr bringing it out of 2nd sp. yrh, and complete the tr. yrh, from the back of work place hook into 2nd sp across the bar of 2nd tr and out of 3rd sp at the back. yrh, and complete the tr. Repeat to end of round finishing with hook under st ch, making a sl st.

Repeat Round 12 6 times. Finish off with 1 row dc.

Scarf

With No 7.00mm hook make 23ch.

Row 1 1tr into 4th ch from hook, 1tr into every st, 2ch.

Row 2 yrh, place hook under bar of 2nd tr, bringing it out of the 2nd sp. yrh, complete tr, repeat st once more. *yrh, place hook behind work and over bar of next st, yrh, complete tr at back. Repeat from * twice more. Repeat to end of row making 3tr to front of work and 3tr to back, 2ch, turn.

Row 3 2tr at back of work, *3tr at front, 3tr at back, repeat from * to end of row, 2ch, turn.

Row 4 As Row 2.

Row 5 As Row 2.

Row 6 As Row 3.

Row 7 As Row 2.

Repeat rows 2 to 7 until scarf is as long as required. Finish with 1 row of tr in every stitch.

Fringe

Cut 88 30cm (12in) lengths of wool. Take 4 lengths together. Put hook through tr sp. Fold lengths in half and pull lp through. Pull ends through lp and tighten. Repeat in every other tr sp. Trim edges straight.

Design 6: Scarf with Pockets and Matching Hat (Lesson 1)
Illustrated in colour on page 94

Materials

300gm each of any yarn of chunky thickness in 2 colours;
No 7.00mm hook

Measurements

The hat will fit an average-size head. The size can be adjusted by working more or less rows. The scarf can be made shorter by making a shorter base chain.

Tension

11st and 6 rows to 10cm (4in)

Design Note

Both hat and scarf are worked sideways making vertical stripes.

Scarf

With colour A make a ch 2m (6½ft) long or larger or shorter if you wish.

Row 1   1tr into 4th ch from hook and tr to end of row. Change to colour B. Break off colour A leaving about 20cm (8in).

Row 2   3ch, tr to end of row. Change to colour A and break off colour B, leaving 20cm (8in).

Work Row 2 11 more times, changing the colour every row.

Pockets (optional)

With colour A make 25ch.

Row 1   1tr into 4th ch from hook, 1tr into every ch.

Change to colour B, 3ch, turn.

Row 2   Work in tr to end of row.

Continue working in tr with 1 row of each colour until 11 rows have been worked.

To Make Up

Place pockets into position at each end of scarf and either sew or double crochet in place.

Fringe

Cut 54 lengths each 25cm (10in) long of each colour. Use 3 lengths together to loop through for the fringe (see Lesson 1, page 19). The ends left at ends of rows can be looped into the fringe.

Hat

With colour A make 33ch.

Row 1   1dc into 2nd ch, 3dc, 4htr, tr to end of row, 3ch, turn.

Row 2   Work tr to last 8st, 4htr, 4dc, change to colour B, 1ch, turn. Rows 1 and 2 form pattern. Work 2 rows of each colour until 32 rows have been worked from the beginning. Finish off leaving a long end for sewing up.

To Make Up

Gather through ends of rows forming centre of hat and sew edges together. Turn back to make a brim.

Design 7· Beret and Stole in Three Colours (Lesson 2)
Illustrated in colour on page 94

Materials
Beret: 1 × 50gm ball Twilleys Capricorn Chunky
Stole: 6 × 50gm balls Twilleys Capricorn Chunky (2 balls of each colour); No 7.00mm and 10.00mm hooks; 70cm (27in) millinery elastic
Measurements
Beret: To fit an average-size head — adjustable with elastic
Stole: 54cm (21in) wide — adjustable length
Tension
Beret: 11st to 10cm (4in)
Stole: 6st to 10cm (4in)

Beret

With No 7.00mm hook make 6ch and sl st into a circle, 3ch.
Round 1 11tr into centre of circle, sl st to top of standing ch (12 bars).
Round 2 1tr into base of tch, 2tr into every st to end of round, sl st to top of tch, 3ch (24 bars).
Round 3 Repeat Round 2 (48 bars).
Round 4 2tr, *2tr into next st, 3tr. Repeat from * to end.
Round 5 2tr, *2tr into next st, 4tr. Repeat from * to end. Finish with 2tr into last st. Sl st to tch, 3ch (36 bars).
Round 6 1tr into every st, sl st to tch, 3ch.
Round 7 As Round 5.
Rounds 8 and 9 As Round 6.
Round 10 Decrease by working 2tr tog for the complete round.
Round 11 1tr into every st, finishing with 1ch.

Round 12 1 round of dc into every st.
Round 13 Sew millinery elastic to fit head. Hold along edge of last crochet round and work 1 round of dc into previous round and over millinery elastic. Run in ends. Decorate with pompom if desired (see Lesson 6, page 85).

Stole

With No 10.00mm hook and colour A make 34ch.
Row 1 yrh, insert hook into 4th ch from hook, yrh and pull through. yrh, pull through 2lps and leave lp on hook. yrh, insert hook into next st, yrh, pull through. yrh, pull through 2lps, yrh, pull through 3lps on hook, 2tr, 2tr into next st, *2ch, 2tr into next st, 2tr, (2tr tog) twice, 2tr, 2tr into next st. Repeat from * once more. 2ch, 2tr into next st, 2tr, 2tr tog, 1tr, change to colour B, 3ch, turn.
Row 2 In 2nd and 3rd st work 2tr tog. 3tr, 1tr into 2ch sp, *2ch 1tr into same 2ch sp, 3tr (2tr tog) twice, 3tr, 1tr into 2ch sp. Repeat from * once more, 2ch, 1tr into 2ch sp. 3tr, 2tr tog, 1tr, change to colour A, 3ch, turn.

Continue with pattern working 1 row of each colour for 33 more rows or until stole is length required.

To Make Up
1 Run in all ends.
2 Make large tassels of 10 strands each 50cm (20in) long in the 3 colours.
3 Attach to points of pattern.

Design 8: Shawl in Picot Stitch *(Lesson 2)*
Illustrated in colour on page 53

Materials
4 × 100gm balls Twilleys Capricorn Chunky; No 8.00mm hook
Measurements
Width: 1.50m (60in)
Length – centre to point: 95cm (37in)
Tension
As this is a lacy pattern it is impossible to give an accurate tension. This is unimportant as the size of the shawl can be determined by the number of rows worked.

Shawl

Make 12ch, sl st into a circle.

Row 1   9ch, miss 3ch (1dc 3ch 1dc) into next ch, miss 3ch, 9ch, 1dc, turn.

Row 2   Sl st along 3ch, 9ch, miss 3ch (1dc 3ch 1dc) into next ch, miss 3ch, 9ch, 1dc, turn.

Row 3   Sl st along 3ch, 9ch, miss 3ch (1dc 3ch 1dc) into next ch, 5ch (1dc 3ch 1dc) into 3rd ch of 9ch, 9ch miss 3ch, 1dc, turn.

Row 4   Sl st along 3ch, 9ch, miss 3ch (1dc 3ch 1dc into next ch, 5ch) twice (1dc 3ch 1dc) into 3rd of 9ch, miss 3ch, 9ch, 1dc, turn. This row forms pattern but work 1 extra (1dc 3ch 1dc 5ch) in every row. Work 23 more rows.

Row 28   7ch, 1dc into 5ch lp, *3ch, 1dc into centre ch of 5ch lp. Repeat from * to end of row. Sl st along 4st, 3ch (first st of edging).

Edging Working along the side.

Row 1   3tr into end st, 1tr into every st to point of shawl. Into centre ch make 1tr 2ch 1tr. Tr along other side taking 3tr into last st, 3ch, turn.

Work 2 rows more as Row 1.

Work 1 row of dc into every st along the longest side taking 3dc into first and last st. 2dc, *5ch, 5dc. Repeat from * to centre point of shawl. Make a 5ch picot at the point and work other side to match. Run in ends and finish off.

Design 9· Summer Cardigan and Suntop in Cotton *(Lesson 2)*
Illustrated in colour on page 43

Materials
Cardigan: 8 (9) × 25gm balls Patons Cotton Top;
Suntop: 4 (5) × 25gm balls Patons Cotton Top; No 3.50mm and 4.00mm hooks
Measurements
Cardigan:
Bust: 91–97 (102–107)cm; 36–38 (40–42)in
Length: 54 (58)cm; 21 (23) in
Sleeve: 20 (25)cm; 8 (10)in
Suntop:
Length 30 (36)cm; 12 (14)in
Tension
16st and 9 rows to 10cm (4in)

Cardigan

Left Back and Front
With No 4.00mm hook make 82 (90) ch.
Row 1 1dc into 2nd ch from hook, 1dc into every ch, 3ch, turn.
Row 2 Miss 2nd st, 1tr into 3rd ch, *1ch, miss 1st, 1tr. Repeat from * to end of row, 3ch, turn.
Row 3 1tr into 2nd st, 1tr into every st to end of row, 3ch, turn.

Rows 2 and 3 form pattern throughout. Work in pattern until 17 (19) rows have been completed from the beginning. Sl st over 32st, 3ch, work in pattern to end of row. Work in pattern for 5 more rows, making 34ch at end of row.

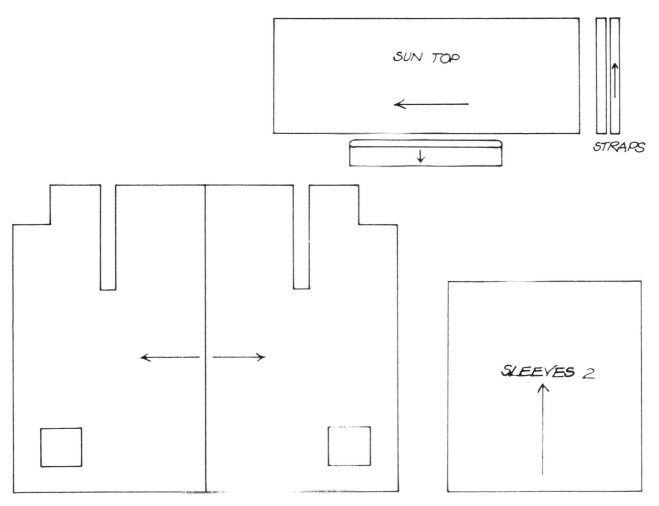

SUN TOP

STRAPS

SLEEVES 2

101

Next row 1tr into 4th ch and pattern to end of row.
Pattern 10 (12) more rows. Sl st over 12st, pattern to end of row.
Work in pattern for 5 more rows. Finish off.

Right Back and Front
Rejoin yarn to base ch at centre back. Work 1 row of dc. Continue working Right Back and Front to match Left Back and Front.

Sleeves (make 2)
Make 31 (39) ch.
Work in pattern for 36 rows and finish off.

Pockets (make 2)
Make 26ch. Work in pattern for 9 rows.

Pocket Edging
1 Work 2 rows dc, 3ch, turn.
2 Work 1 row of 1tr, 1ch, miss 1st, finishing with 1tr.
3 Work 2 more rows of dc.
4 Fold over so that the trs and sp make picots.
5 Sew into position and sew pockets on to jacket.

To Make Up
1 Sew shoulder seams.
2 Sew top of sleeve to straight armhole edge.
3 Sew sleeve seam from bottom towards armhole until it exactly fits the underarm seam and sew under arm.

Edging
1 Start at centre back of neck. Work 2 rows of dc along neck, down left front, across bottom, up right front, joining with a sl st at centre back of neck, increasing 3 into 1 at top and bottom corners of front and decreasing 2 into 1 on neck curve.
2 Work 1 row of 1tr, 1ch, miss 1st.
3 Work 2 more rows of dc, decreasing over the increases and increasing over the decreases on Row 1. Fold back and sew into position.
4 Repeat edging to match on bottom of sleeves.

Suntop

With No 4.00mm hook make 30 (38) ch.
Row 1 1tr into 4th ch from hook, tr to end of row.

Continue working in tr until work measures 81 (91)cm; 32 (36)in. Sew up last row to the base chain.

Welt
Row 1 Attach yarn to seam. With No 3.50mm hook, 3ch, work 1 row of tr into side of every row, sl st to top of tch, 3ch, turn.
Row 2 *yrh, place hook under 2nd tr, yrh and complete tr. Place hook at back, yrh, insert hook over bar of 3rd tr, yrh and complete st. Repeat from * to end of row. Continue with this rib stitch for 10 (12) rows (see Lesson 1, page 18).

Top Edging
Attach yarn to top edge and with No 4.00mm hook work 1 row of dc, 1 row of (1tr, 1ch, miss 1st) and 1 row of dc. Finish off.

Straps
Make 1 row of ch as long as you would like the straps to be. Work to match the top edging and sew into place.

Design 10: Man's Sweater (Lesson 2)
Illustrated in colour on page 71

Materials
23 (24, 25) × 50gm balls Patons Capstan for Aran knitting; No 6.00mm and 7.00mm hooks

Measurements
Chest: 97 (102, 107)cm; 38 (40, 42)in
Length: 68 (73, 76)cm; 26½ (28½, 30)in
Sleeve length: 59cm (65, 69)cm; 23½ (25½, 27)in
Note: Larger sizes are in brackets. When there are no brackets in the instructions all sizes are worked the same.

Tension
13 st to 10cm (4in)
10 rows to 10cm (4in)

Design Note
All ribs are worked sideways in double crochet with a No 6.00mm hook. The textured pattern is worked entirely in raised trebles.

Back
With No 6.00mm hook make 16ch.
Row 1 1dc into 2nd ch, 1dc into every ch, 1ch, turn.
Row 2 1dc into back lp of 2nd dc of previous row. Work dc into back of each st to end of Row 1 taking 1dc into the tch, 1ch turn. This row forms the rib. Repeat Row 2 53 (57, 61) times.

With No 7.00mm hook turn work sideways to form ribbing. 3tch for 1st tr.
Row 1 Crochet in tr along side of ribbing strip. Take 2st in each of the 1st 4 rows and again 2st in each of last 4 rows, 2ch turn. This gives 61 (65, 69) st.
Row 2 yrh, place hook under bar of 2nd st, yrh and complete the tr (RtrF), yrh, bring hook from back of work in front of 3rd tr and out to back, yrh and complete the tr (RtrB). Continue working 1RtrF and 1RtrB to end of row finishing with 1RtrF under tch of previous row, 2ch turn.
Row 3 Repeat Row 2.
Row 4 1RtrB, 1RtrF, repeat to end of row finishing with 1RtrB under tch of previous row.
Row 5 Repeat Row 4.

Rows 2 to 5 form basket stitch pattern worked throughout. Continue until work measures 42 (45, 48)cm; 16½ (17½, 18)in. Decrease for armhole. Omit tch on previous row. Sl st along 8 (8, 9)st, 2tch. Continue in stitch pattern along row until there are 8 (8, 9) st left, 2ch, turn.

Continue in pattern until work measures 68 (73, 76)cm; 26½ (28½, 30)in. Finish off.

Front
Work in pattern exactly the same as for Back until 12 (13, 14) rows after the armhole shaping.
Neck Shaping Work in pattern over 16 (17, 18) st, 2ch, turn.
Next row Decrease 1st by working 2nd and 3rd st together. Pattern to end of row, 2ch, turn.
Next row Decrease 1st at end of row, 2ch, turn. Work until right side measures same as Back. Finish off.

Turn to left side of neck shaping. Miss 9 (11, 11) st, rejoin yarn, 2ch. Decrease by working 2st together. Work in pattern to end of row.
Next row Work in pattern to end of row, decreasing 1st at end, 2ch, turn.
Work to match other side. Finish off.

Sleeves
With No 6.00mm hook make 16ch.
Work rib as for bottom of sweater for 27 rows, 3ch. Turn rib sideways.
Row 1 With No 7.00mm hook work 1 row of tr into ends of ribbing rows, increasing 4 (5, 6) st at each end of 1st row of tr making 35 (37, 38) tr bars.
Continue in pattern increasing 1st at each end of every 3 rows until there are 59 (63, 67) st. Continue in pattern until sleeve measures 59 (65, 69)cm; 23½ (25½, 27)in including cuff. Finish off.

Polo Neck
With No 6.00mm hook make 26ch. Work in rib st for 55 (58, 61) rows. Fold in half placing base ch along the last row. Crochet both rows together in dc to make a circle. Finish off.

To Make Up
Block into shape but do not press. Sew up in the following order:
1 Shoulder seams; 2 Head of sleeve to straight edge of armhole; 3 Side seams; 4 Start sewing sleeve from wrist to armhole. Sew seam until there is just enough left to fit underarm space. Sew underarm seam and finish off.

Pin join of polo neck to centre back of neck. Pin centre front to centre half of polo and sew in place with a firm but not too tight stitch (it must be large enough for the head to pass through). If seams need pressing use a dry cloth and warm iron.

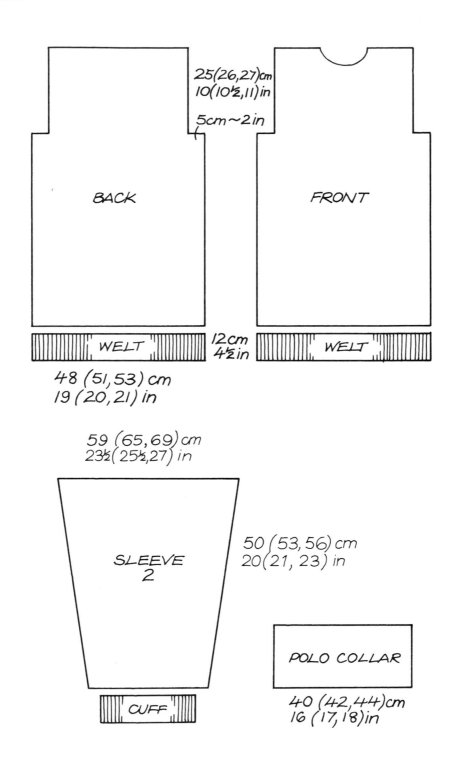

25(26,27)cm
10(10½,11)in

5cm ~ 2in

BACK

FRONT

WELT

12cm
4½in

WELT

48 (51,53) cm
19 (20,21) in

59 (65,69) cm
23½(25½,27) in

SLEEVE
2

50 (53,56) cm
20(21, 23) in

CUFF

POLO COLLAR

40 (42,44)cm
16 (17,18)in

Design 11: Textured Jumper in Three Colours (Lesson 2)
Illustrated in colour on page 54

Materials
12 × 50gm balls Phildar Pegase (4 balls each of 3 colours – any 4 ply yarn can be used); No 5.00mm hook
Measurements
Bust: 87 (92, 97)cm; 34 (36, 38)in
Sleeve length: 46 (47, 48)cm; 18 (18½, 19)in
Length: 54 (56, 58)cm; 21 (22, 23)in
Tension
18st and 14 rows to 10cm (4in)

Design Note
The shape is simple. The textured fabric looks difficult but it is produced by a very easy stitch worked in three colours – one row of each colour.

Stitch Pattern and Colour Sequence
Row 1   (colour A) Work in tr.
Row 2   (colour B) Work in dc.
Row 3   (colour C) * 1dtr under bar of tr of previous tr row, 1tr. Repeat from * to end of row.

Rows 2 and 3 form pattern.

Back and Front (both alike)
With colour A make 77 (83, 89)ch.
Row 1   1tr into 4th ch from hook, 1tr into every st to end

of row. Change to colour B, 1ch, turn.
Rows 2 and 3   As in stitch pattern.
Continue working in stitch pattern and colour sequence until work measures 37 (39, 42)cm; 14½ (15½, 16½)in, from the beginning.

To Shape Armholes
Sl st over 6 (8,10) st and leave same number unworked at other end of row. Change colour, 1ch, turn. Continue in stitch pattern and colour sequence until armhole measures 19 (20, 22)cm; 7½ (8, 8½)in. Finish off.

Sleeves
With colour A make 62 (66, 70) ch.
Work in pattern and colour sequence for 46 (47, 48)cm; 18 (18½, 19)in.

To Make Up
1   Sew shoulder seams for 8cm (3in).
2   Place centre of sleeve head to shoulder seam and sew in place
3   Sew up side seams; sew sleeve seams.

Tie Belt
Using double yarn make 2ch 1dc 1ch, turn. 1dc into side of st, 1ch, turn. Continue until tie belt is 1.50m (60in) long.

Design 12: Jacket in Bouclé Yarn *(Lesson 2)*
Illustrated in colour on page 84

Materials
12 × 50gm balls Sirdar Romano or Georges Picaud Fifi or Pingouin Bouclette Imprimée; 1 × 50gm ball of contrast chunky yarn of a plain colour; No 6.00mm or 7.00mm, 8.00mm, 9.00mm hooks

Measurements
Bust: 92 (97, 102)cm; 36 (38, 40)in
Sleeve length: 46 (47, 48)cm; 18 (18½, 19)in

Tension
9 st and 5 rows to 10cm (4in) with No 9.00mm hook

Design Note
The jacket is made with treble stitch throughout and the sizes altered only by the size of hook.

Back and 2 Fronts *(worked together)*
For size 91cm (36in) use No 7.00mm hook; 97cm (38in) use No 8.00mm hook; 102cm (40in) use No 9.00mm hook. Make 92ch.
Row 1 1tr into 4th ch from hook, 1tr into every st, 3ch, turn. Repeat this row 6 times more.
Row 8 (Pocket openings) 1tr into 2nd tr, 6tr, 12ch, miss 12st, 50tr, 12ch, miss 12st, 8tr, 3ch, turn.
Row 9 1tr into 2nd tr, continue row in tr working across ch sts of previous row, 3ch, turn. Continue until work measures 38 (41, 44)cm; 15 (16, 17)in, more if a longer jacket is required.

To Divide for Armholes
Row 1 1tr into 2nd tr, 16tr to end of row, 3ch, turn. Continue on these 18tr for 7 more rows. Sl st across 5st, continue row with 3ch, 12tr, 3ch turn. Work 1 row tr and finish off.

Back Yoke
Return to bottom of armhole, miss 8tr, attach yarn, 3ch, 37tr, 3ch, turn. Work 9 more rows and finish off.

Left Yoke
Return to left armhole, miss 8tr and work to match right side.

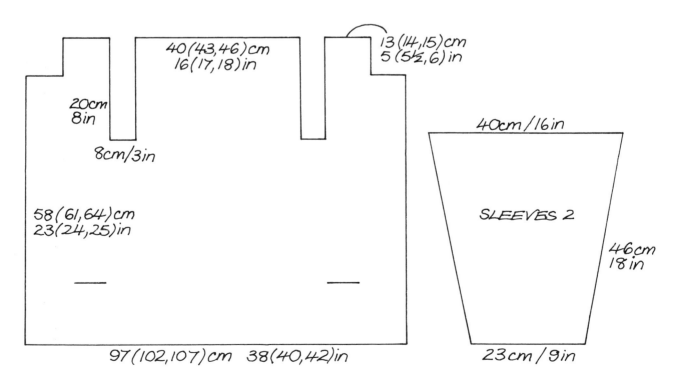

Sleeves

The sleeves are worked from the top towards the wrist, enabling the length to be altered easily. Make 38ch.

Row 1 1tr into 4th ch, 1tr into every ch (36tr), 3ch, turn. Continue working in tr, decreasing 1st at each end of every 3rd row until 24tr remain. Finish off when sleeve measures 46cm (18in).

To Make Up

1 Sew both shoulder seams.
2 Place top of sleeve to straight edge of armhole and sew.
3 Sew sleeve seam (both sides) to 8tr of underarm and continue along sleeve seam.

Decorative Edging

Row 1 With No 7.00mm (6.00mm) hook start at centre back of neck, attach yarn, 1ch and work dc round the neck, down left front, across back and up right front, taking 3dc into top and bottom corners of fronts, sl st to the 1ch.

Row 2 Attach contrast wool to Row 1. 2ch, 1htr, *yrh, place hook in between htr and ch, yrh pull through, repeat from * 3 times, yrh and pull through all the lps making a puff st, miss 1dc. Repeat this st all round jacket. Finish off.

Row 3 With original yarn work 2dc in between every puff st. Finish off at back of neck with sl st. Work edging round bottom of sleeves.

Pockets

1 Attach yarn to top edge of pocket. Work 12tr for 6 rows. Finish off and sew in place.
2 On right side attach yarn to front edge of pocket, work 1 row dc and finish off.
3 Attach contrast yarn and work 8 puff st as on jacket edging. Finish off.
4 Attach main colour and work 1 row dc. Finish off. Sew edging into place at each side.

To Finish

Run in all ends. Press jacket under a dry cloth with a warm iron.

Alternative Edgings

1 Work 3 rows of dc, 1 row of crab st (page 77, Fig 89) on front lps of dc and 1 row of dc on back lp of st.
2 Work 4 rows of dc in contrasting colours.

Design 13: Batwing Jumper and Matching Hat *(Lesson 2)*
Illustrated in colour on page 42

Materials
Jumper: 10 × 50gm balls Georges Picaud Sport Picaud; 6 × 50gm balls Pingouin Bouclette Imprimée; No 6.00mm and 7.00mm hooks
Measurements
Bust: 87–97cm (34–38in)
Length: 49cm (19in)
Sleeve (length from neck to cuff): 74cm (29in)
Tension
14st and 5½ rows to 10cm (4in) in Sport Picaud
9st and 5 rows to 10cm (4in) in Bouclette Imprimée

Jumper

Back
With Bouclette Imprimée and No 7.00mm hook make 22ch.
Row 1 1tr into 4th ch from hook. 1tr into every ch to end of row, 3ch, turn.
Row 2 1tr into 2nd tr, 1tr into every st including standing ch at end of row. Continue as for Row 2 increasing at each end of every 3rd row until 20 rows from the beginning.

To Shape Neck
Tr over 7st and finish off. Rejoin yarn and tr over last 7st. Finish off.

Front
Work as for Back until 17 rows have been completed.

To Shape Neck
Tr over 8st (9 bars with standing ch), 3ch, turn. Work 3 more rows decreasing at neck edge twice. Finish off. Rejoin yarn to last 9tr at other side of neck and work to match. Sew shoulder seams together.

Batwing Sleeves
Row 1 Join Bouclette Imprimée to front waist edge and along the side of rows up the front and down to back waist. Work 80dc and finish off.
Row 2 Join Sport Picaud to beginning of previous row,

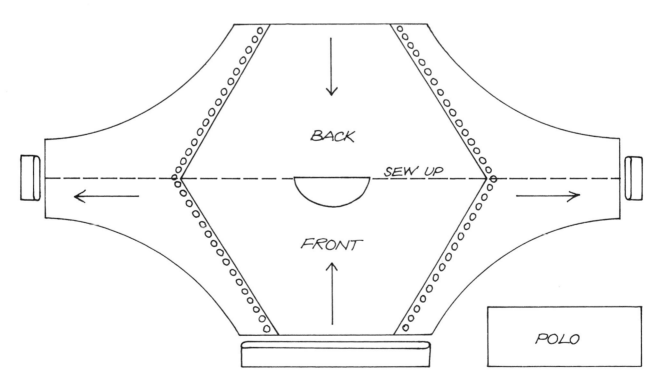

3ch, miss 1dc, 1htr * yrh, place hook sideways into sp of side of htr, yrh and pull through. Repeat from * twice more, yrh and pull through the 7lps on hook, yrh and pull through, miss 2dc, 1htr. Repeat from * to end of row.

Row 3   With Bouclette Imprimée take 1dc into 1st st of Row 1, 2dc into every sp between the puff st to end of row. Finish off yarn and join in Sport Picaud.

Rows 4 to 8   3ch, 1tr into back lp of every st to end of row. Continue in pattern working tr into back lp of previous row. Decrease 2st each end of row for 5 rows and 1 each end of every row until 30st remain. Finish off.

Work other sleeve in the same manner.

To Make Up
Fold right sides together and sew up sleeves and sides down to waist.

Waistband
With Sport Picaud and No 6.00mm hook make 15ch.

Row 1   1dc into 2nd ch, dc to end of row, 1dc, turn (clockwise).

Row 2   Into back of lp of 2nd dc, 1dc, dc into back lps to end of row, including standing ch of previous row, 1ch, turn. Repeat this row 92 times.

Join into a circle by working 1 row of dc into base of 1st row. Sew to waist of jumper.

Polo Neck
With Sport Picaud and No 6.00mm hook make 20ch. Work 54 rows as for waistband and join into a circle. Sew to neck edge.

Cuffs (make 2)
With Sport Picaud make 12ch. Work 26 rows as for waistband and join into circle. Sew to bottom of sleeves. Press with cool iron under dry cloth.

Hat

With No 7.00mm hook and Sport Picaud make 6ch, sl st into a circle.

Round 1   3ch, 11tr into centre of circle, sl st to top of standing ch (12trs).

Round 2   3ch, 1tr into base of ch, 2tr into each st, sl st to top of standing ch (24trs).

Round 3   3ch, work as for Round 2 (48trs).

Continue working straight without any increasing for 9 rounds. Always complete each round with a sl st to top of standing ch. Change to Bouclette Imprimée and work 6 rounds more. Finish off.

Design 14: Blouson Jacket in Three Colours (Lesson 2)
Illustrated in colour on page 81

Materials
Phildar Pegase (Aran thickness)
6 × 50gm balls of grey (colour A); 4 × 50gm balls of petrol (colour B); 4 × 50gm balls of old rose (colour C); No 6.00mm and 5.00mm hooks; 12 buttons

Measurements
Bust: 87–92 (97–102)cm; 34–36 (38–40)in

Tension
12st and 14 rows to 10cm (4in)

Design Note
The jacket is worked entirely in double crochet, inserting the hook into the back of the loop. This forms the ribs which are crocheted on to the waist and sleeves. The garment is worked sideways, starting at the centre back. The only two seams sewn up are the underarm side seam and sleeve seam. The pattern for this garment is shown on page 114.

Right Back
With No 6.00mm hook and colour A make 61 (65)ch.
Row 1 1dc into 2nd ch, dc to end (60 [64]ch), 1ch, turn.
Row 2 With colour B work dc into back of each st to end of row, 1ch, turn.
Row 3 With colour C repeat Row 2.

Carry yarn along the side and work 1 row of each colour to form the striped pattern. Work until 8 rows have been completed from the beginning and leave on one side.

Right Front
With colour C make 49 (53)ch.
Work 6 rows in pattern and make 12ch at end of last row. Leave on one side and return to Right Back.

Right Back and Front
Work in pattern along Back, the ch st added to Front, and across Front. Continue in pattern for 18 (24) rows.

To Decrease for Side Seam
Sl st along 10st and continue in pattern to last 10st, 1ch, turn. Decrease 3st at each end of every row 7 (8) times until 58 (60)st remain. Continue working in pattern and colour sequence decreasing 1st each end of every row until there are 38 (40)st. Work 30 rows more.

Design 21: Multi-coloured Tunisian Jacket (page 123)

To Decrease for Cuff

1dc into 2nd st, *work 2dc tog, 1dc. Repeat from * to end of row.

Left Back and Front

Return to original base ch of centre back. Work 1 row of dc with colour A into base ch.

Work Left Back and Front to match right side, finishing off at left cuff.

Waistband

With colour A make 15ch.

Row 1 1dc into 2nd ch and dc to end of row, 1ch, turn.

Row 2 1dc into back lp of 2nd st, dc to end of row working into back of every lp. Continue working this dc rib st for 96 (104) rows.

Cuffs

With colour A work 28 rows as for waistband. Join into a circle by working into back of dc and base ch together. Finish off.

Collar

With colour A make 25ch. Work as for waistband.

To Make Up

1   Sew underarm and sleeve seams.

2   Work 1 row of dc in colour A around bottom edge at waist.

3   Pin waistband into position and dc, working into band and garment together, on right side.

4   Attach collar and cuffs in the same way.

Front Edging

Left side

With right side facing, working in dc with colour A, start at left side of collar, and work along collar and the Left Front to bottom of waistband. Work 3 more rows and finish off.

Right Side

Row 1   With colour A start at waist with right side facing and work along to edge of collar.

Row 2   Work 1 row dc finishing at waist.

Row 3   2 (4)dc, 2ch, miss 2st, 6dc to end of row, finishing with 3 (5)dc (12 buttonholes).

Row 4   1 row of dc into every st. Finish off. Sew on buttons and work round buttonholes to strengthen.

Design 15: Evening Jumper in Mohair and Lurex (page 115); Design 2: Lurex Evening Top and Matching Bag (page 91); Design 16: Stole in Broomstick Crochet (page 116) – a close-up of this stitch pattern is shown on page 41

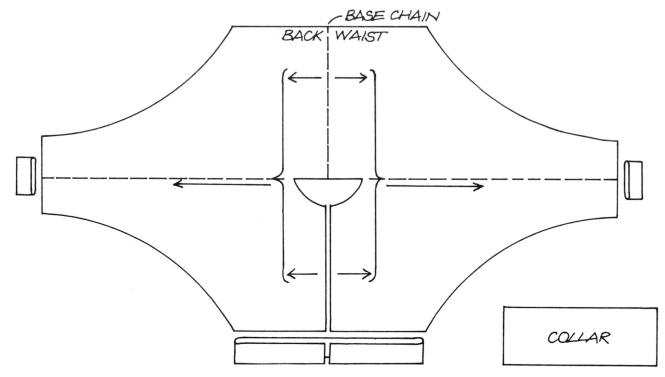

Design 14

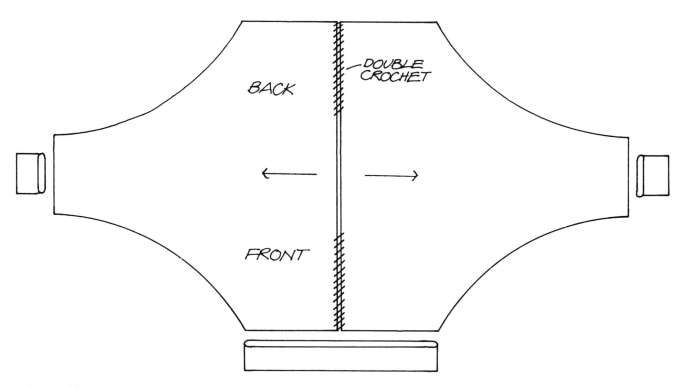

Design 15

Design 15: Evening Jumper in Mohair and Lurex (Lesson 2)
Illustrated in colour on page 112

Materials

9 × 40gm balls Georges Picaud No 1 Kid Mohair; 1 ball Lurex Feu d'Artifice; No 6.00 and 7.00mm hooks

Measurements

Length: 34cm (21in)
Sleeve length from neck to wrist: 60cm (24in)

Tension

10st and 6 rows to 10cm (4in)

Design Note

The jumper is worked sideways in two pieces making half the front and half the back and one sleeve together. The two halves are crocheted together in double crochet with a lurex yarn at the centre back and centre front. The back and fronts are interchangeable and the deep V can be at the back or the front. The pattern is for one size but this can be made larger by working more rows before decreasing for the sleeves and by making a larger waistband.

Half Back, Half Front and 1 sleeve (make 2)

Make 92ch.

Row 1 1tr into 4th ch from hook, 1tr into every ch, 3ch, turn.

Row 2 1tr into 2nd st, 1tr into every st to end of row, 1tr into tch, 3ch, turn. Repeat this row 14 times.

To Decrease for Side Seam and Sleeves

Omit 3ch on last row, sl st over 6st, 3ch, tr to 6st before end of row. 3ch, turn.

Work 1 row without decreasing. Decrease 2st at each end of next 10 rows and decrease 1st at each end of next 4 rows. Continue working until work measures 50cm (19in).

Work second side to match.

Edging

With No 6.00mm hook work 1 row of dc into base ch of centre front and centre back. Work 2 more rows of dc.

Change to Lurex yarn and work 1 row of spike st as follows: *insert hook into st 1 row down, complete dc, insert hook into next st 2 rows down, complete dc, insert hook into st 3 rows down, complete dc, insert hook into st

2 rows down complete dc. Repeat from * to end of edging. Work edge to match on 2nd side.

To Join the Two Sides

Continuing with Lurex yarn place edgings together and work dc into st of both sides for 30st, making sure that the spike st match on both sides. Then on one side only work 40dc. Finish off end. Reverse work and start at the other edge. Crochet both sides together with dc for 20st, then work dc on one side to 1st join. Finish off.

Decoration

1 With neck edge facing fold back along edge of third treble row.

2 Insert hook through the spaces between the 2 treble rows and work 1 row of dc in Lurex extending from front waist to back waist. Finish off.

3 After the next 3 rows of treble, fold back and work another row of dc. Repeat once more (3 rows of 'tucking').

This dc row in Lurex on the surface of the garment makes an attractive design of zigzags. Turn work round and work to match on other side of garment.

Waistband

With mohair yarn and No 6.00mm hook make 15ch.

Row 1 1dc into 2nd ch from hook, dc to end of row, 1ch, turn.

Row 2 1dc into 2nd st, 1dc to end of row, 1dc into tch. Repeat this row 84 times. Join into a circle by working 1 row of dc into the base ch.

Cuffs (make 2)

Make 12ch. Work as for waistband for 26 rows. Join by working 1 row into base ch.

To Make Up

1 Run in all ends.

2 Sew side seams.

3 Work 1 row of dc around bottom edge inserting hook into side of rows and taking 2st tog all round.

4 Attach waistband by working into jumper edge and waistband with another round of dc.

5 Attach cuffs in the same way.

Design 16: Stole in Broomstick Crochet *(Lesson 4)*
Illustrated in colour on page 112

Materials

5 × 50gm balls 4 ply or Mohair yarn; 1 broomstick or 25mm (1in) diameter knitting needle; No 6.00mm hook

Stole

With No 6.00mm hook make 60ch.

Row 1   Place last lp on to broomstick. Pull lps through every ch (60lps).

Row 2   Remove lps. Work 2lps together with 2dc to end of row (30lps).

Row 3   Place last lp on to broomstick. Insert hook into back of 2nd st and pull through. Repeat to end of row. Continue in Broomstick Crochet until stole is as long as required.

Fringe

Cut 240 pieces of yarn 40cm (16in) long (wind round a piece of cardboard or an old book). Take 4 lengths together, fold in half, pull lp through a 'broomstick group' and with crochet hook pull ends through lp and tighten. Continue fringe along the edge.

Work other end to match and trim fringe. Do not press.

Design 17. Shawl In Broomstick Crochet *(Lesson 4)*

Materials

5 × 100gm balls Twilleys Capricorn Chunky; No 6.00mm hook, 1 broomstick or 25mm (1in) diameter knitting needle

Note It is possible to use any yarn but the amount required may vary

Shawl

Make 5ch.

Row 1   Draw through 5lps.

Row 2   Remove lps from broomstick with 10dc.

Row 3   Draw through 10lps.

Row 4   *Remove 5lps from broomstick with 10dc. Repeat from * once more.

Row 5   Draw through 1lp in every dc (20lps).

Row 6   Remove first 5lps from broomstick with 10dc, remove groups of 5lps with 5dc until last group. Work 10dc into last group.

Repeat this row until shawl is as large as required.

Fringe

Make fringe along the sides. Cut yarn into 40cm (16in) strips. Use 4 lengths together, fold in half and with hook pull lps through 'broomstick group'. Pull ends through and trim fringe. Do not press.

Broomstick Edging as an Alternative

Row 1   Work along the two sides and round the point with 1dc into end of each row, followed by a 3ch lp.

Row 2   Pick up broomstick lps into every st. Finish off in the usual way removing lps on next row.

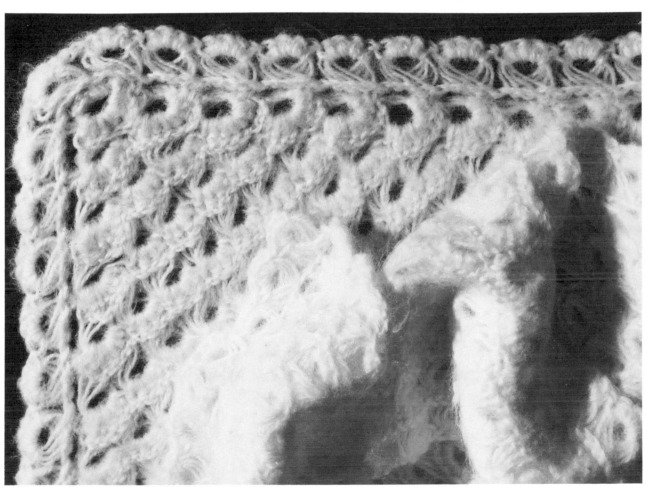

Design 18: Broomstick Crochet Waistcoat *(Lesson 4)*

Illustrated in colour on page 83

Materials

5 × 50gm balls chunky yarn in main shade; 3 × 50gm balls in contrasting shade; 3 buttons; 1 25mm (1in) broomstick; No 7.00mm hook

Measurements

Bust: 91cm (36in)

Length: 54cm (21in)

Abbreviations

MS = main shade; C = contrasting shade

Tension

15lps and 3 rows of broomstick lps to 10cm (4in)

Half Back and Front (make 2)

Make 125ch. Slip last ch lp on to broomstick. Work 6 complete rows of broomstick lps in alternate colours. Fold in half and dc edges together leaving 20cm (8in) unworked for armhole. Make 2nd side to match.

Neck Edging (MS)

On right side attach yarn to 1st base ch. Make 15ch, work dc along this ch continuing in base ch to other end, 1ch, turn.

Next row   dc to end of row, 1ch, turn.

Next row   (Make buttonholes) 2dc, *2ch, miss 2st, 4dc*. Repeat from * twice more, dc to end of row, 1ch, turn.

Next row   dc to end of row and finish off.

Repeat on left side without buttonholes.

Centre Back Seam (MS)

Crochet both centre backs together with dc for 31cm (12in).

Waistband

Work 1 row tr along bottom edge. Work a tr rib in raised trebles (RtrF and RtrB [see Lesson 1, page 18]). Sew edging to waistband on both sides. Sew on 3 buttons.

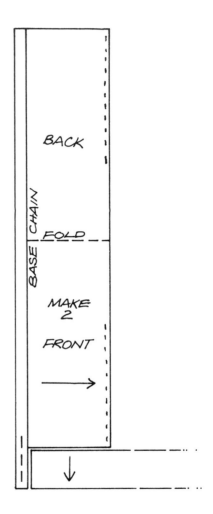

Design 19. Jacket and Waistcoat in Tunisian Crochet *(Lesson 5)*
Illustrated in colour on page 82

Materials

7(8) × 100gm balls Twilleys Capricorn Chunky in brown (colour A)

4(5) × 100gm balls Twilleys Capricorn Chunky in peach (colour B)

No 7.00mm hook; No 7.00mm or 8.00mm Tunisian hook

Measurements

Bust: 87–91 (97–102)cm; 34–36 (38–40)in

Length: 61 (66)cm; 24 (26)in

Sleeve: 46cm (18in)

Tension

12 (11)st to 10cm (4in). 3 patterns to 10cm (4in). Instructions for size 97–102cm (38–40in) are worked with No 8.00mm Tunisian hook.

Design Note

The jacket is worked sideways from centre back and centre front to the side. The colour change is always on the left of the work for the return row giving a woven effect.

Back

With Tunisian hook No 7.00mm (8.00mm) and colour A work 79ch.

Row 1 yrh, insert hook into 4th ch, yrh, pull through lp, yrh, pull through 2lps, yrh, draw through 1lp leaving this lp on hook. Repeat this st into every ch leaving the last lp on hook (76 bars). Do not turn.

Row 2 (Colour B) yrh, draw through 1lp, *yrh, draw through 2lps. Repeat from * to end of row leaving 1lp on hook. These 2 rows make Tunisian treble.

Row 3 Insert hook into 2nd vertical lp of previous row, *yrh, draw through, leave lp on hook, repeat from * into every vertical lp to end of row.

Row 4 Pick up colour A and work return row as Row 2. Rows 3 and 4 make Tunisian double crochet.

Repeat 4-row pattern 6 times.

41 (43)cm 16(17)in

20cm 8in

4cm 1½in

61 (66)cm 24(26)in

BACK

FRONT 2

46cm/18in

SLEEVES 2 (WORKED SIDEWAYS)

49 (51)cm / 19 (20)in

→ ARROW SHOWS DIRECTION OF WORKING

Note Always miss the first vertical loop but take care not to miss the last stitch of the outward row. Do not turn work. The right side is always facing. Continue with colour sequence.

To Shape Left Armhole

Sl st along vertical lps of previous row over 28st. Work in Row 3 pattern (Tunisian dc) to end of row (48st). Repeat 1 row Ttr and 1 row Tdc. Sl st along vertical lps to cast off.

Rejoin yarn to right side of centre back (colour A). Start with 3ch and work 1 row of Ttr into base ch. Continue in pattern and colour change as for other side to armhole shaping.

To Shape Right Armhole

Work 48st in pattern (Tdc), sl st into vertical lps of previous row 28 times. Break off yarn and rejoin to armhole edge for return row. Work 1 row Ttr and 1 row Tdc. Sl st along vertical lps to cast off.

Left Front

With colour A, make 71ch. Working into 4th ch from hook work 2 complete patterns (8 rows). Attach 8ch to end of row and work 1 row Ttr finishing across the ch. This makes neck shaping. Work return row. Work 1 row Tdc and then 3 complete patterns.

To Shape Armhole

Work 48st in Tdc, sl st into vertical lps of previous row 28 times. Break off yarn and rejoin to armhole edge for return row. Work 1 pattern. Sl st along vertical lps to cast off.

Right Front

Work as for Left Front but make shapings at opposite ends of work.

Sleeves (2 worked sideways)

With colour A and Tunisian hook No 7.00mm (8.00mm) make 67ch.
Repeat pattern and colour change 14 times. Sl st into vertical lp of previous row to cast off.

Pockets (make 2)

With colour A make 24ch. 1Ttr into 4th ch and Ttr into every ch to end. Continue in pattern until 3 patterns have been completed.
With colour A and No 7.00mm hook work 3 rows of dc finishing at left of pocket. On front lp of dc work 1 row of dc from left to right (crab st, see page 76). Work 1 row of dc into back of dc lps, making 2 rows into 1 row of lps to make a 'corded' edge.

To Make Up

1   Sew shoulder seams and side seams.
2   Place straight edge of sleeve along straight edge of armhole and sew into position.
3   Sew sleeve seam leaving 4cm (1½in) open at top to sew to underarm.
4   Pin pockets in position and sew.

Jacket Edging

Join colour A to centre-back neck, 1ch. Work in dc all round jacket edging joining with sl st to 1ch. Starting with 1ch work 3 more rows of dc increasing 3st into 1 at top and bottom corners of both fronts and decreasing 2st each side on neck curve. Work corded edging as on pocket. Make edging on bottom of sleeve to match jacket.

Waistcoat

Work as for jacket without sleeves. Make edging to match jacket round armhole edges.

Design 20: Tunisian Coat, Hat and Scarf (Lesson 5)
Illustrated in colour on page 93

Materials

Coat: 15 × 100gm balls Georges Picaud Dorothée Bis; No 8.00mm hook; No 10mm Tunisian hook; 6 buttons

Hat and Scarf: 3 × 100gm balls Georges Picaud Dorothée Bis

Measurements

Bust: 81–87 (92–97)cm; 32–34 (36–38)in
Sleeve length: 46 (49)cm; 18 (19)in
Length: 107 (112)cm; 42 (44)in

Tension

12st, 4 Tunisian rows and 4 return rows to 10cm (4in)

Design Note

The coat is worked lengthways from the centre back to the side and from the centre front to the side. The sleeves are also worked sideways. Instructions are given for a matching scarf but this is not illustrated.

Coat

Left Back

With No 10 Tunisian hook make 120 (126)ch.
Row 1   1Tdc into 2nd ch from hook, Tdc to end of row.
Row 2   yrh, pull through 1st, *yrh, pull through 2lps. Repeat from * to end of row (Tunisian return row), 3ch.
Row 3   *yrh, insert hook from right to left through vertical lp. yrh, pull through 1lp, yrh, pull through 2lps, yrh, pull through 1lp. Leave lp on hook. Repeat from * to end of row (Ttr).
Row 4   As Row 2.
Row 5   Insert hook into 2nd vertical lp, yrh, pull through. Repeat Tdc to end of row.
Row 6   As Row 2.

Rows 3 to 6 form pattern worked throughout. Continue in pattern until 20 (24) rows or 10 (12) double rows have been worked.

To Shape for Armhole

Sl st over 24 (26)st and continue row in Tdc. Continue in pattern for 5 more rows finishing at the armhole edge. Sl st over 20st, 20dc, Ttr to end of row. Work 1 Tunisian return row.

Next row   Sl st over 25st. Tdc to end of row. Work 1 Tunisian return row. Sl st along row to cast off.

Rejoin yarn to base ch (right side). Working from the hemline to the neck and starting with 1 row of Tdc, work right side to match left side.

Right Front

Make 110 (116)ch.
Row 1   3ch, 1Ttr into 4th ch. Ttr to end of row.
Row 2   Tunisian return row.
Row 3   Tdc.
Row 4   Tunisian return row.
Row 5   Ttr.
Row 6   Tunisian return row ending with 10ch.
Row 7   Tdc into 10ch, work to end of row in Tdc. Work until 18 (22) rows have been completed.

To Shape Armhole

Sl st over 24 (26)st. Complete armhole and side shaping as for Back.

Left Front

Work to match Right Front for 6 rows.
Row 7   With spare yarn attach 10ch to end of row. Work in Tdc across row and the 10ch which shape neck. Continue working as for Right Front.

Sleeves

Make 54 (60)ch. Work in pattern for 42 (46) rows. Sl st along row to finish off.

Front Edgings
Left Front

With No 8mm hook work 3 rows of dc. Work crab stitch (see Lesson 6, page 76) from left to right into front lp of st.
Next row   Work 1 row of dc into back lp, behind crab st. Finish off.

Right Front

Work as for Left Front but on 2nd row work buttonholes as follows: from neck edge work 3dc, *3ch, miss 3st, 8dc. Repeat from * 5 more times, dc to end of row.
Next row   dc to end of row.
Last row   1 row of crab st on front of lp and 1 row of dc into back of lp. Finish off.

Pockets (make 2)

Work 20ch.

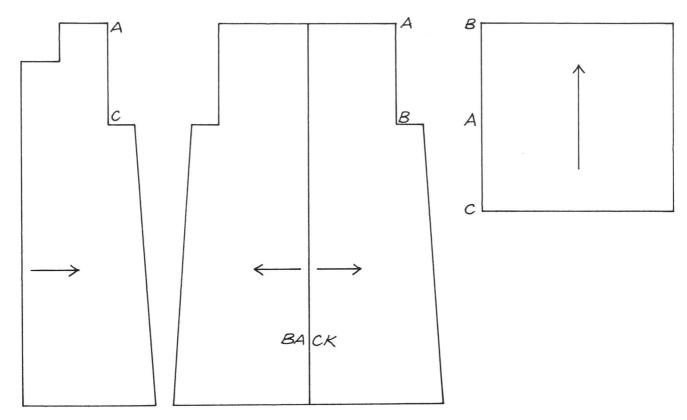

Row 1 Tdc to end of row.
Work in pattern until 12 double rows have been completed.

Change to No 8.00mm hook and ordinary crochet, work 4 rows of dc with crab st edging to match Front.

To Make Up
1 Sew up shoulder seams.
2 Work edging in dc round neck for 6 rows.
3 Complete with edging in crab st as for Front.
4 Place centre of sleeve head to shoulder seam and sew sleeve head into armhole.
5 Sew side seams.
6 Sew sleeve seams until end of sleeve fits underarm.
7 Sew patch pockets on to front.
8 Work edging on sleeves to match front edging.
9 Work 1 row of dc along hemline.
10 Sew on 6 buttons (Dorset buttons – see Lesson 6, page 79).

Belt
Make 5ch. Work in plain Tunisian stitch (see Lesson 5, page 68), working always into 1st st which gives a diagonal effect. Work dc round two large plastic rings and sew to ends of belt.

Hat
With No 8.00mm hook make 6ch, sl st into circle, 3ch.
Round 1 11tr into circle, sl st to tch, 3ch.
Round 2 2tr into every st, 1tr next to tch, 3ch.
Round 3 As Round 2 (48 bars)
Round 4 yrh, *1RtrF, 1RtrB. Repeat from * to end of round, sl st to top of tch, 2ch.

Repeat Round 4 8 more times.
Next 2 Rows Work dc.
Last Row Work crab st from left to right. Finish off.

Scarf
Make 24ch.
Row 1 yrh twice, 1dtr into 5th ch from hook, dtr to end of row, 3ch, turn.

Work in pattern as for hat but using dtr throughout instead of tr until scarf is as long as required.

Design 21: Multi-coloured Tunisian Jacket *(Lesson 5)*
Illustrated in colour on page 111

Materials

5 × 50gm balls of the main shade which is used for edgings as well as stripes; 800gm of various textures and colours (those illustrated were mohair, chunky and double knitting from Georges Pecaud, Twilleys, Patons and Phildar); No 7.00mm hook; No 8.00mm Tunisian hook

Measurements

Bust: 81–87 (92–97)cm; 32–34 (36–38)in
Length: 61 (66)cm; 24 (26)in
Sleeve seam: 46 (51)cm; 18 (20)in

Abbreviations and Stitches

See Lesson 5, page 67

Tension

12 Tunisian st to 10cm (4in)

Design Note

If you make this jacket it will be your interpretation of this design. Choose a selection of yarns of various colours and textures which you would like to use together and either blend or contrast your colours. Choose your own order of Tunisian stitches and work within the framework of the measurements given in the pattern. The colours are changed on the left side of the work and only two rows are worked in one colour. A list of the stitches used is given but not in the order worked so whatever you do it will be your interpretation of this shape and therefore quite exclusive.

Back and Fronts

Note The jacket is worked in one piece to the armholes. Using No 8.00mm Tunisian hook and colour of your choice make 111 (119)ch.

Row 1   Work into 2nd ch 1Tdc. Tdc to end of row.

Row 2   Change colour and work the Tunisian return row: yrh, pull through 1lp, *yrh pull through 2lps. Repeat from * to end of row. Every alternate row is worked in this way with a new colour.

Continue working with any of the following stitches (for further details, see Lesson 5): Tunisian dc; Tunisian tr; Tunisian p; Tunisian dropped tr (Tdtr), ie 1 Tdtr 3Tdc or 2 Tdtr 2p; Tunisian bobble (Tb), ie 1 Tb 3Tdc.

Work until there are 14cm (5½in) from beginning and set aside after a return row.

Pockets (make 2)

Make 15 (16)ch with No 8.00mm hook and work in same colours and stitches as used for main garment. Return to main garment. Work 10 Tdc, place pocket into position behind work, right side of pocket to wrong side of jacket, and continue across pocket piece for 15 (16)st. Returning to main garment work until there are 25 (26)st left. Place second pocket in place and work across pocket and then across main garment to end of row.

Continue until work measures 39 (43)cm; 15 (17)in from beginning.

To Divide for Yokes

Start at right edge with Tdc row. Work across 23 (24)st. Sl st over 8 (9), work 48 (50)st, sl st 8 (9)st, work 23 (24)st to end of row. The sl sts form bottom of armhole.

Left Front

Continue in the stitch and colour of your choice until work measures 51 (56)cm; 20 (22)in from beginning, finishing with a Tunisian return row.

Neck Shaping

In Tdc work 16 (17)st, sl st 7st to end of row. Join next colour and work on the 16 (17)st until work measures 59 (64)cm; 23 (25)in from beginning.

Work 1 row of sl st to cast off.

Back Yoke

Work rows in same stitches and colours to match Left Front. With new colour work the return row on centre 48 (50)st. Continue straight until it matches Left Front in length, colour and stitch.

Work 1 row of sl st to cast off.

Right Yoke

Work as for left yoke. Sl st across 7st at beginning of row for neck shaping.

Work 1 row of sl st to cast off.

Sleeves

Work to match main part of jacket in colour and stitch. With No 8.00mm hook make 28 (32)ch. Increase 1st at each end of row every 5cm (2in) until there are 46 (52)st. Continue until work measures 46 (51)cm; 18 (20)in. Work 1 row of sl st into every st. Fasten off.

To Make Up

1 Run in all ends.

2 With No 7.00mm hook crochet shoulder seams with dc.

3 Place centre of sleeve to shoulder seam, pin into position.

4 With sleeve facing work 1 row of dc.

5 Sew sleeve seams and pocket linings in position.

Edgings

Work the edging of your choice in main shade (see Lesson 6). Edge all round jacket not forgetting increases, 3st into 1 at the corners. Edge bottom of sleeves and top of pocket. Do not press.

APPENDIX 1
HOOK SIZES

UK	US	UK	US
0.60mm	14 steel	4.00mm	F
0.75mm	12 steel	4.50mm	G
1.00mm	10 steel	5.00mm	H
1.25mm	8 steel	5.50mm	H
1.50mm	7 steel	6.00mm	I
1.75mm	4 steel	7.00mm	K
2.00mm	0	8.00mm	11 wood
2.50mm	B	9.00mm	13 wood
3.00mm	C	10.00mm	15 wood
3.50mm	E		

APPENDIX 2
EQUIPMENT

Basic materials
A selection of hooks of different sizes
Yarns of different textures

In addition you will need
Tunisian hooks
Large needles for Broomstick Crochet
Hairpins

To measure
A tape measure with inches on one side and centimetres
on the other
A ruler

Sewing up
Large wool needles
Bodkin
Pins with glass knobs

Pressing
Iron
Pressing surface (large old table) prepared with thick
blanket and cover
Pressing cloth of cotton or muslin
Sleeve board
Padded shapes

Pattern making
Cutting scissors
Large sheets of paper
Calculator
Notebook
Pencil and felt-tips

APPENDIX 3
LIST OF SUPPLIERS

(Yarns are available in good department stores throughout the country)

Mail Order Firms
R. S. Duncan & Co
Falcon Mills
Barton Lane
Bradford BD7 4OJ

John Lewis Partnership Ltd
Oxford Street
London W1

William Hall & Co Ltd
177 Stanley Road
Cheadle
Cheshire SJ8 6RF

The Silver Thimble
33 Gay Street
Bath BA1 2NT

The Yarn Store
The Studios
54 Vartry Road
London N15

Mailyarns Ltd
1122 Melton Road
Syston
Leicester

The following firms have helped by kindly donating yarn for some of the garments:

Dave and Mary Vinall
Woolscope
South Street
Chichester
W Sussex
(suppliers of Georges Picaud yarns and Tunisian hooks)

Georges Picaud of Paris
c/o Priory Yarns Ltd
48 Station Road
Ossett
W Yorks

Patons and Baldwins Ltd
McMuillen Road
Darlington
Co Durham DL1 1YQ

H. G. Twilley Ltd
Roman Mill
Stamford
Lincolnshire PE9 1BG

Phildar (UK) Ltd
4 Gambrel Road
Westgate Industrial Estate
Northampton NN5 5NF

For list of suppliers of Tunisian hooks:

Aero Needles Group PLC
Box No 2
Edward Street
Redditch
Worcs B97 6HB

Broomsticks (wooden) supplied by:

M. Kent
1 Orchard Street
Chichester
W Sussex PO19 1DD

126

INDEX